p√

INTELLECTUAL IMPAIRMENT

362.3
H432i

INTELLECTUAL IMPAIRMENT

The battle against handicap

Alastair Heron

Professor Emeritus,
University of Melbourne, Australia

Mary Myers

Consultant Psychiatrist (Mental Handicap)
Sheffield Health Authority, UK

ACADEMIC PRESS, INC.

(Harcourt Brace Jovanovich, Publishers)

London   Orlando   San Diego   New York
Toronto   Montreal   Sydney   Tokyo

ACADEMIC PRESS INC. (LONDON) LTD
24/28 Oval Road,
London NW1 7DX

United States Edition published by
ACADEMIC PRESS, INC.
Orlando, Florida 32887

British Library Cataloguing in Publication Data
Heron, Alastair
    Intellectual impairment.
    1. Mentally handicapped persons
    I. Title   II. Myers, Mary
    362.3   HV3004

    ISBN 0-12-342680-4

    LCCCN: 82-82941

PRINTED IN THE UNITED STATES OF AMERICA

85 86 87 88   9 8 7 6 5 4 3 2

Foreword

At least 40 million people all over the world are thought to be intellectually impaired. Most of them live in rural areas and are without services. Of those who live in towns and cities, only a minority have access to schools, housing or jobs.

Intellectual impairment presents us with a global challenge. We need to look beyond plans and policies for our own country and our own community and try to work in closer partnership with people in other countries, to share ideas and experiences and to learn from one another. This is not just a matter of developed countries reaching out and sharing their experiences with less developed countries, nor of seeking to export methods and models from one culture to another. It involves international collaboration in coming to an understanding of what we have in common, and how we can benefit from one another's failures as well as successes. In looking at ways in which other countries try, succeed or fail to meet the needs of people with intellectual impairments, we may be able to come to a better understanding of our own efforts.

This book provides an excellent point of departure for such a journey. We set off in what appear to be familiar surroundings by looking at services in our own country but are soon made aware of the gap between the rhetoric and the reality, between what we would like to do and what we can actually achieve. The obstacles we face cannot be overcome merely with money, though it is tempting to blame our failings and our frustrations on the meanness of governments and local authorities. Visitors from developing countries can sometimes be seen smiling politely when they hear us complaining about shortage of money. They must be wondering what they could achieve with what to them must seem colossal sums of money that we already spend.

The obstacles we face are not all easily visible. Of course, the anachronistic buildings that we have inherited from our predecessors are all too visible, but what about the dilemma of choosing between improving the quality of life of those who live in them and pulling them down so that we can develop residential alternatives outside hospital? And how do we feel about some of the buildings that we have only just built or that are still on the drawing board—for example, the 96-bedded hospitals that are now held up as models of domestic-style

v

accommodation, in some of which there are no facilities for residents to be able to make tea or cook snacks? And what do we know about the quality of life and care in our local authority hostels? How many of their residents would be able to live with support in sheltered or ordinary housing?

The fact is that the many millions of pounds that are spent every year on services for intellectually impaired people are inexorably tied to our struggle to maintain a minimum standard of service for many people who are spending their days and nights in patterns of service provision that are no longer appropriate to today's philosophies and policies. The obstacles to the development of locally based and fully comprehensive services lie largely in the assumptions made by those of our fellow citizens whom we elect to make decisions about people with disabilities, the relative degree of priority which is to be accorded to meeting their needs—assumptions concerning their ability to learn to live in ordinary houses, attend ordinary schools, be trained to work and use community leisure and recreational facilities.

How do we escape from this dilemma? We can continue with the well-tried British formula of incrementalism—painfully adapting and improving our existing services until they begin to resemble the kind of service we want to see. We could study the North American de-institutionalization movement, with its continuous use of litigation and the courts to ensure the civil rights of minority groups. We can also examine the radical Italian approach of closing all special schools and institutions by act of parliament and almost overnight placing their inhabitants into ordinary classrooms and houses. We can study how other countries not unlike our own organize their services and whether there are lessons to be drawn from their experience.

But it is when we turn to the Third World that we begin to realize not only how much all countries have in common but how much developed countries could learn from the Third World. While we are struggling to improve anachronistic services and develop more appropriate community models, Third World countries are for the most part starting from little or nothing—no special schools, hospitals, sheltered workshops, or staff trained specifically for work with intellectually impaired people. Third World countries are not faced with the choice between improving or dismantling inappropriate services or with balancing the equation of resource allocation between old and new. They are in the fortunate position of being able to start with a clean slate and from first principles.

Perhaps it is no coincidence that it is precisely at this point that we find a common meeting point between developed and developing countries. Both are aiming to develop local decentralized services; to provide access to the ordinary services available to all other local citizens—to use primary care workers, whether these are health, social welfare or community workers, and to build on their basic training with additional knowledge and skills needed to support families in helping their impaired child to acquire basic daily living skills. Developed countries are at last beginning to learn that it is better to take the service to the client than to ask the client to travel to a centralized service. The success and popularity of home visiting programmes such as "Portage" with families is matched by the professional discovery that it is possible to train almost anyone to become a competent home visitor in a matter of days, provided that continuous support and professional back-up are available and the home visitor is not left to work in isolation.

"Portage" and other home visiting programmes have been adapted to the needs of many countries, for example in South America, the Caribbean and Asia, and have been used by community workers without any special training in impairment. Such programmes provide support and encouragement to families by showing them it is possible to take positive steps to assist the development of impaired children and that the methods are comparatively simple and straightforward.

The WHO manuals "Training the Disabled in the Community" represent another radical and innovative approach to training ordinary locally-based community workers to work with families in meeting basic needs of impaired children and adults. Similarly, developing countries without a highly developed special school system can plan to integrate impaired children into the ordinary school system and provide the necessary support services to teachers. However limited the educational resources of a developing country for normally developing children, attempts are being made to ensure that as many impaired children as possible are included in whatever facilities are available. In some cases, positive discrimination is invoked to give priority to children with special needs. Finally, countries without specialized residential institutions and hospitals are increasingly trying to ensure that people with disabilities remain in the community, living in houses similar to those used by others.

Reading the resolutions, declarations and speeches which were issued during the International Year of Disabled Persons leaves one with the impression that most governments and international organizations are committed in principle to the goals of community living and integration for people with impairments and disabilities, and that the twin aims of equality and participation are generally agreed. Whether these global aims can be realized depends partly on the allocation of resources but much more on the will to succeed, on favourable attitudes from the public at large, on effective collaboration between professionals and parents and on the involvement of people with disabilities.

This book provides a masterly overview of both national and international developments and offers sound constructive advice on how we can all learn from one another to provide the kind of service which will meet the needs of people with intellectual impairments and help to promote their integration into the local community as full citizens.

September 1982   Peter Mittler
Professor of Special Education,
University of Manchester

Preface

We approach the problem of intellectual disability from the same philosophical basis and with a strong consensus about ways and means, yet from sharply differing backgrounds and experience which will we hope combine in a strongly complementary way. One of us—a lifespan developmental psychologist with no previous first-hand knowledge of services for intellectually disabled people—was given in 1975 the challenging opportunity to carry out a unique evaluation of such services in a large urban area, over a period of five years. During approximately the same period, the other—a psychiatrist with a longstanding interest in people with these disabilities—was engaged from 1974 in setting up in an adjoining urban area a community-orientated "mental handicap" service under the newly reorganized National Health Service in England.

For one, the task was to understand the problems faced by those who planned, managed and delivered the services, and by those who were at the receiving end: those who are intellectually and multiply disabled, of all ages, and their parents and relatives. For the other, the task was to start with the needs of the individual and to organize and provide a network of services with relatively limited resources. From two different but contemporaneous points of departure, and along different avenues of experience, we came independently to identical conclusions about a philosophy of approach, and to overlapping and complementary insights about how such a philosophy should be translated into practical programmes in a variety of real-life situations.

We have chosen to set the stage, so to speak, for our joint approach to questions of philosophy and practice by starting with the needs of the individual and the course of their development from birth onwards. With the interests and problems of readers from a wide range of national systems very much in mind, we describe and examine a variety of existing structural models of service delivery, before making use of the insights gained from a unique large-scale evaluation of one major attempt to provide a comprehensive service. Some of those insights are salutary.

The stage thus set, we can turn to ends and means, in a positive and forward-looking spirit, citing recent examples of innovation and creative problem-solving on the part of service providers within both the public and voluntary sectors. Particular attention is paid to the new

ix

roles and responsibilities of the latter, as the needs of the intellectually disabled person are met more and more within the community instead of institutionally. Inevitably many of our "examples of good practice" are drawn from the country in which we live and work, but we have also drawn upon our knowledge of what has been achieved elsewhere, either at first-hand or from the unpublished accounts of colleagues who have worked or made visits abroad.

Finally, we try to face realistically the immense and daunting problems faced by those who live in that majority of countries which can only be perceived as poor, by comparison with those in Europe, North America and Australasia. In so doing we hope to dissuade them from making some of our mistakes, but also to learn from their endeavours.

By now it will, we trust, be reasonably clear that we have not set out to write a conventional textbook on the provision of care, residential or otherwise, to those children and adults who are to varying degrees disabled by intellectual impairment, with or without associated physical problems. Our primary aim is to focus attention on the needs—and ways of meeting them—of people who have traditionally been treated as if they were chronically sick. We hope to encourage those with a "health" background—and those being trained within such a setting—to perceive most intellectually disabled persons as ordinary people who may need health services from time to time, just like the rest of us. A minority of them will have one or more enduring physical, physiological or psychological conditions which require accurate diagnosis, appropriate treatment, and—in some cases—frequent monitoring and specialist attention.

We hope to arouse a positive interest in this professionally-neglected group of our fellow citizens on the part of such professionals as psychologists; speech, occupational and physiotherapists; orthodontists, audiologists and optometrists; and—last but emphatically not least—community physicians, community nurses and health visitors: the primary care team.

The more that intellectually disabled children live in their own homes or those of foster parents, and that intellectually disabled adults move to (or stay in) ordinary accommodation in the community, the more important will become the understanding and support of schoolteachers, adult educators and social workers. But the success of their efforts to reduce the handicaps resulting from intellectual disabilities will largely depend on a growing understanding on the part of neighbours, shopkeepers, public transport workers—and the community at large. The greatest single obstacle to a good life for the intellectually disabled person is without question the attitudes of his or her fellow citizens. Anything that can help to make these more understanding, more accepting, less affected by inaccurate folklore and unfounded fears, will enhance the life prospects of those who are intellectually impaired—and more handicapped than they need to be.

June 1982   Alastair Heron
                                                               Mary Myers

Professor Heron's present address: 19 King Ecgbert Road, Sheffield S17 3QQ, U.K.

Contents

CHAPTER 1

Introduction

The Problem of Terminology

There can be few topics so bedevilled by semantic difficulties as that to which this book is addressed. Of the two major international bodies in the field, one is committed to the scientific study of *mental deficiency* while the other brings together in a league all the national societies for the *mentally handicapped*. This latter term is now in general use within the United Kingdom, despite the fact that Britain still has *mental subnormality* hospitals and special schools for the *educationally subnormal*. In Canada, the USA, and some parts of Australia the term in general use is *mental retardation*; but in New Zealand and other parts of Australia public services and voluntary bodies have adopted the expression *intellectual handicap*.

During the International Year of the Disabled Person in 1981, considerable emphasis was placed on the desirability of distinguishing between impairment, disability and handicap, and of referring to persons rather than to categories. While it was generally agreed that ordinary public usage would cause reference to "the impaired person" to be somewhat puzzling, it was stressed that while disablement was a direct result of the impairment of one or more functions, the degree to which a person is handicapped is frequently determined, in part, by external factors of an educational or social nature. We are convinced that continued use of the adjective "mental" has become undesirable, mainly because confusion with mental illness reinforces fear and prejudice among members of the public. There is plenty of day-to-day evidence for this, including the apparently incorrigible tendency of media subeditors to delete the word "handicap" when headlining a report which refers to a hospital or other unit for the "mentally handicapped". It then becomes a "mental hospital", which for a majority of the general public still means something like a lunatic asylum. Hence our decision to advance the use of "intellectual" as the preferred—and technically accurate—adjective. Since we are wholly in accordance with the principle that people as individuals, not impersonal categories, have needs which should be met, the remaining

1

question of terminology turns on the choice between "disabled" and "handicapped".

The point noted above—that "handicap" can and frequently does involve educational and social factors—is in our view a valid one. In the UK and some other countries, a person with a congenital or otherwise permanent intellectual impairment is eligible for a disability pension, but two equally impaired adults both officially accepted as being disabled persons may not be equally "handicapped". For example, one may be a long-stay resident in a hospital or hostel with little or no regular contact with life in the general community, while the other may dwell in an ordinary house and interact frequently with neighbours and those whom he or she meets in ordinary public places of recreation or entertainment. It is therefore part of our approach and argument that it is the way in which, and the extent to which, the needs of the intellectually impaired and thereby disabled person are or are not met, that determines the degree to which he or she is handicapped. This position is fully consistent with the arguments set out in "The International Classification of Impairments, Disabilities and Handicaps", originally published for trial purposes as long ago as 1976, and now available in a revised version (WHO, 1980). The three terms are defined as follows.

Impairment. In the context of health experience, an impairment is any loss or abnormality of psychological, physiological or anatomical structure or function.

Disability. A disability is any restriction or lack (resulting from an impairment) of ability to perform an activity in the manner or within the range considered normal for a human being.

Handicap. A handicap is a disadvantage for an individual, resulting from an impairment or a disability, that limits or prevents the fulfilment of a role that is normal (depending on age, sex, and social and cultural factors) for that individual.

In the discussion of the relationship between these three concepts, the WHO manual displays a welcome concern with the very practicalities to which we have drawn attention (pp. 32–33).

> Although too much can be made of the importance of semantic distinctions, the acid-test for a preferred nomenclature is whether it promotes practical benefits. The latter should come about as a clearer description of processes reveals to what extent and in what way problems may be

solved. Considerable care has been applied to the selection of descriptive terms in this manual, so as to reinforce the conceptual distinctions. This effort can be seen at two levels.

(i) Avoidance of the same word to identify an impairment, a disability and a handicap. In colloquial speech there has been a trend to euphemism, with words being debased as mental retardation first became mental disability and then mental handicap. This succeeds only in blurring the distinctions; the disadvantage experienced by individuals with psychological impairments can vary, so that it is inappropriate to refer to a handicap as "mental". Thus the descriptive adjectives "mental" and "physical" may correctly be applied to impairments, but their use in relation to disabilities is loose and to handicaps quite unsuitable. It is perhaps vain to hope that the tide of careless usage can be reversed, but at least in serious discourse the logic of terminology should be exploited to reinforce the conceptual framework.

(ii) In addition to seeking different descriptive terms, the use of different parts of speech also seemed to be appropriate. Thus for the qualities represented by impairments an adjective derived from a substantive is apposite, but for the activities included as disabilities a participle was deemed more suitable, the "-ing" ending emphasising the dynamic aspect. An exhaustive consistency in this regard has not been possible, but a trend should be apparent. These points can best be illustrated with examples:

Impairment	Disability	Handicap
language	speaking	
hearing	listening	orientation
vision	seeing	
skeletal	dressing, feeding	physical independence
	walking	mobility
psychological	behaving	social integration

In our attempts to follow these precepts, we have endeavoured to be consistent in our usage, not always finding this easy. So far as we are aware, the expression "intellectually *handicapped* person (child, adult)" has not been used by us in this volume, since its use would beg the question to which we are addressed. When writing about an "impairment" or "an intellectually-impaired child" little difficulty arises; we have found it harder to decide with adults, but have allowed the context to determine whether "impaired" or "disabled" is more suitable. In the terms of the WHO proposed usage, we find "intellectually disabled" to be most often the expression of choice. Finally, it is necessary to add that quotations from other sources have not been altered; the necessity to leave them as they are in fact provides eloquent testimony to the contemporary confusion. In this volume we must confine our attention to the needs of those whose impairment was evident at birth or became so within a year or two. But a good deal of what we wish to discuss may also apply to those whose impairment was the result of later damage, from whatever cause, to a previously intact brain.

The Contemporary Scene

Although in the technologically and industrially more developed countries, most intellectually disabled persons live in the homes of their parents—even well into middle life or later—the next most likely place to find them is in some form of institution. The decade of the 1970s saw a trend towards "de-institutionalization" of the intellectually disabled, following nearly twenty years behind a similar movement in respect of those who are mentally ill. But for those—especially adults—who were intellectually disabled, the new trend frequently meant only a movement out of large institutions, frequently isolated, into mini-institutions such as small hospitals or units attached to general or psychiatric hospitals, or into "hostels" typically accommodating 20–24 residents.

A notable example of this was launched in 1971, and provides the basis for the detailed evaluation described in Chapter 4. Whether under public or voluntary auspices, similar developments took place in many countries during the decade—and this trend has not yet ceased. A similar movement towards universal educational provisions within the legal school age-limits was accompanied by pressures for "integration" as contrasted with special schools and classes. Undue haste in both these movements—most notable in the USA—often led to unsatisfactory or even disastrous outcomes. Increasing dissatisfaction has also been expressed with the inadequate and "dead-end" character of much after-school provision through adult training centres, sheltered workshops, and activity therapy centres.

During the same decade of the seventies, but on a much smaller scale, an approach based on a fundamentally different philosophy was simultaneously being demonstrated and slowly winning understanding and support. Put simply, this parallel development started with the recognition that children and adults who were intellectually impaired had an entitlement to live and to be served in the community, not as a category of the chronically sick but as ordinary people whose learning capacity was limited—to varying degrees—by their impairments. The principle is stated succinctly in the title of a recent book, *People Not Patients* (Mittler, 1979). In Chapter 5 of this volume, examples are provided of this principle in practice. It would be unwise to underestimate the difficulties involved in taking the next step, from the mini-institutions of the 1970s to the "ordinary life" of the 1990s and beyond.

In the first place, as we show in a later chapter, many countries already possess a well-developed service structure—whether wholly public, partly voluntary or, as in the case of The Netherlands, wholly voluntary but state-supported. Change in the direction of the "ordinary life" principle will, to varying extents in these different systems, require legislative and administrative change. This can—and often does—take a long time and a great deal of effort to bring about. Secondly, existing service systems already involve considerable numbers of professional workers, all dependent—as they understandably perceive it—on a continuance of the system within which they work. They will have to be convinced that there is a meaningful and fulfilling new role for them in a different system—client-centred, community-based, non-institutional.

Thirdly, the anxieties of parents and relatives must be taken very seriously. As individuals and as families, and also in the organizations to which they belong whether locally, regionally or nationally, they seek *security* for their intellectually disabled relatives. Whatever the admitted shortcomings of the institutional provisions, whether "traditional" or "modern", large or small, they represent a kind of security with which an alternative "ordinary life in the community, with whatever support is needed" must be seen to compare favourably. Finally, we are forced to recognize squarely the problems posed by the attitudes of most citizens towards their intellectually-impaired fellows. These vary from culture to culture, and from time to time and place to place within a culture. But there is one near-universal element: human beings are made uneasy by appearance and/or behaviour which is atypical. There is, however, abundant evidence that they can learn to accept these differences, but once again, the process may be slow and difficult to achieve.

Against this background, it is salutary to recognize that in those countries where the majority of the world's population are to be found, an organized response to the problems arising from intellectual impairment is, of necessity, in its earliest stage. Our concern, as we bring this volume to a close, is that the experience of error in the so-called "developed" countries should not be re-enacted in the Third World. It may have been economically necessary for technology and the supporting educational models to be imported from us: the same necessity cannot be said to apply to the topic with which we are here concerned. It is our hope that mutual learning can characterize the process of service development in the immediate future, as we move towards community and they start from it.

CHAPTER 2

The Evolution of Needs

Human needs vary over a lifespan, and so do the added special needs of people with impairments. They will therefore be considered in chronological order.

The primary need is clearly the prevention of disabilities. This is an enormous field. The physical and mental health of future parents, genetic counselling, varieties of antenatal screening, the prevention of prenatal infections, control of maternal metabolic and nutritional disorders, improved obstetric, postnatal and infant care and nutrition are all recognized as urgent needs capable of being met, given political will and resources. This book, however, is not about primary prevention, but about the needs, ordinary and special, of those people who survive the early biological insults and are left with intellectual and additional impairments.

The chances of survival for a very impaired child remain below those of other children. Living conditions associated with high levels of morbidity and mortality will of course reduce the prospects for an impaired child to almost nil, but survival is dependent on more than available physical facilities. The right of an impaired child to survival is still not totally accepted; in 1981, the International Year of Disabled Persons, British law courts were the scene of debates on the rights to survival of two children because they each had an extra chromosome in their cells (i.e. Down's Syndrome). The World Health Organization defines handicap as "a disadvantage resulting from an impairment or disability that limits or prevents the fulfilment of a role that is normal (depending on age, sex, social and cultural factors) for that individual" (1980). The major handicap or disadvantage of being a devalued person in society is displayed in the continuing debate on the rights of impaired children.

WHO's definition of handicap according to expected social roles is a reminder that the same impairment or disability may not result in the same handicaps or problems in different cultures. The birth of a child with Down's Syndrome may or may not produce all the same handicaps in an extended rural family in Asia, as it does in a nuclear family in urban Britain. The expectations, pressures, and resources within and without the family are likely to be very different. Because of the complexity of varied cultural expectations, the needs to be discussed in this chapter are those of developmentally intellectually impaired people living in the industrialized western world.

The term intellectual impairment covers a wide meaning, without discrimination between such functions as memory, attention span, language or spatial abilities. Where intellectual impairment exists from early in life, commonly there are other associated biological impairments to learning, the effect of which may be present from birth, or may remain latent, to intrude on learning experiences later. For example, the rubella-damaged infant has severe hearing and visual problems to compound his learning difficulties from the start, while the child with Down's Syndrome is at risk of developing catarrhal deafness and short sight insidiously during later stages of growth.

The earliest of impairments, temporary or permanent, demands screening and constant awareness, if resultant disability and handicap are to be kept to a minimum. Tremendous gains have been achieved in the past decade in understanding the prevention, identification and treatment of disorders which produce intellectual and other impairments in children.

Identification and Early Intervention

Child–parent–child dynamics and needs

A small number of major intellectually disabling conditions are recognizable at birth. They include Down's Syndrome, microcephaly and gross neural tube defects. Such conditions may be associated with other physical disorders of, for example, the heart or the senses, requiring the relevant paediatric management. If, however, the child is otherwise physically fit, for the first few months the child's principal need is for the usual ingredients of good infant care. The predominant needs to be met initially may be those of the *parents* in their grief and complex emotional responses to their new situation. The quality of their continuing adjustments to their child and his disabilities will influence the subsequent development of every member of the family unit.

The Needs of the Parents

The recognition, indeed even the suspicion, of disordered development introduces a new dimension to the child–parent relationship. Impairment in a child results in grief, the mourning of the "perfect" child of whom the family are bereft. Grief and mourning contain anger, rejection, guilt, loneliness, sorrow, despair. Whether major impairment is recognized at birth or later, the bereavement is experienced.

Down's Syndrome is the commonest single condition underlying intellectual impairment, and is recognizable at birth. The views of affected parents suggest that telling them together of the diagnosis, on the second day, by a sensitive specialist is the optimum way of starting the major support programme. The parents experience all phases of bereavement. They undergo conflict, in feeling rejection for the "alien" baby, while protective towards its vulnerability. The strength of their rejection and protectiveness varies in time, and between couples, and with the strength of these same conflicting responses in the social environment, which extends from the maternity and paediatric ward staff, to grandparents, and society at large. The first few weeks for such parents in their new knowledge are usually profoundly lonely, with a sense of launching totally unprepared on an uncharted ocean. The despair of their bereavement can be intensified by the muddle of low expectations of "mongols" among both the public and many health professionals. Most newly affected parents, whilst in need of professional advice and counselling, experience great comfort and reassurance from other parents in the same situation. The offer of such support should be provided locally at the very earliest opportunity.

Doctors are sometimes still reluctant to recognize the major help which affected parents may bring to one another, or to take it seriously. The time at which newly-affected parents want to meet others varies, and the opportunity to do so must remain open.

The widely varying rates at which "severely mentally handicapped" children develop demands sensitivity in the organization of parental self-help activities. The child with Down's Syndrome may show in mere months achievements for which his multiply handicapped contemporary takes two years or more. Parents of very "brain damaged" children may find the comparisons too painful, and gain greater comfort from other parents who also have to set very small goals and long time scales. The opportunity to share the special experiences, the slow achievements, to express safely anger and laughter about a subject frightening to outsiders, is of tremendous value to many parents (and wonderful training for professional helpers!). In the absence of other additional support however, even this, in the past, has occasionally become addictive, and some older parents' lives have developed to contain nothing else but the social world of mental handicap—"chronic Mencap-itis" as one parent described it.

Parental adjustments to their growing child with his accumulating achievements and changing handicaps will change too. The attitudes of both father and mother have roots in their past experiences, and their expectations of childhood, parenthood, family life, society and disability. The attitudes and influences of grandparents can have a powerful effect on the parents, and merit attention from the support services. Although usually grandparents provide much comfort and help, the occasional overt or covert rejection of the handicapped child by its grandparents indicates the deep pain they also experience, and family counselling should be undertaken in an attempt to relieve the destructive conflict engendered. Most families accommodate their disabled members lovingly and healthily, but professional work with intellectually disabled adults and their families provides many examples of family pathology; the stunting of personal growth and development in parents, in the disabled person, and in the siblings, which can develop and deteriorate over the years. The parents of thirty years ago (and many younger ones still) received no informed help with their problems in child management, with uncertainty over realistic expectations, or in coping with resentment and conflict about parental roles and responsibilities. For many the professional labelling of the "mentally handicapped" person as having "a permanent mental age of 7", whatever the length of life experienced by them, ensured for them a subsequent life of incompetence and inexperience while their parents continued devotedly in their early controlling role, at times bewildered by the emergence of sexuality and self-assertion in the young adult.

Chronic parental anxiety arising out of previous realistic fears for the child's survival, or more rarely, from deeply-repressed feelings of rejection towards the child, may engender a very high level of parental protectiveness. ("Over-protectiveness" is a very hazardous value judgement). Such high protectiveness, like chronic despair, is likely to result in understimulation of the child, with lost learning opportunities. Such negative feelings are not immutable, and demand sensitive counselling.

By definition, the intellectually impaired individual is a very slow learner; that is the nature of their disability. Their learning will need structure, and positive reinforcement. But parents themselves have similar needs in learning an unfamiliar variety of parenthood, and they too are in great need of positive reinforcement of their efforts. In assessing the child's problems, the professionals must constantly and sincerely focus the parents' attention on the development of latent *abilities*, rather than regularly concentrating on the *disability*. They must do this in such a way as to avoid either undue despair, or gross overexpectations. One sensitive paediatrician taught his juniors "Never take away from a parent with your right hand, without having something to give them in your left hand".

The counselling and advice, therefore, to young parents should contain experience, information and reassurance on the predictable order of developmental progress, with gentle warnings of possible limitations, and acknowledgement of many uncertainties—as with all children. There is a great need to teach parents how to select realistic, achievable, small short-term goals with the methods necessary to reach them, and with clear recording of the results. Parents may need reminding to compare their child's progress against his own earlier performance, and not against other children's. With an only child, a reminder may be necessary that some difficulties can be normal characteristics of childhood itself, and not due to disability.

In the occasional situation where parents find their intellectually disabled child difficult to accept or manage, sensitive counselling must be accompanied by practical advice and help which enables the child himself to become some reward to the parents for their efforts. An enjoyable child is the finest positive reinforcer of good parental behaviour!

The Needs of Impaired Young Children

During the first few years of any child's life, there evolve the exceedingly complex interactions between a rapidly enlarging body with its maturing nervous system and muscular strength, and the immediate environment over which the child is gaining awareness and some control. Each new behaviour exhibited by the young child in one area of development is the foundation for further progress in another area; bodily maturation, varied external stimulation and increments in skills, all enhance global development. An intact child acquires hand–eye coordination, which enables him later to use fine manipulation, which in turn is needed later for discriminatory activities with the shapes and colours of bricks. Early childhood should consist of a harmonious incremental interrelated progression of gross and fine motor abilities, vision, hearing, social and communication skills, and emotional and cognitive development. Cognition is the ability to remember, to see and hear likenesses and differences, to determine relationships between ideas and things. This harmonious development demands both intact maturing faculties, and the environmental opportunities in which to exercise them. During the first two years of life, play and exploration with the simplest of toys contributes to the development of hand–eye coordination, discrimination of form, texture, taste, colour, sounds, temperature, and weight; towards such concepts as liquidity, gravity and constancy. At the same time, the child is developing a sense of his own individuality, his own body shape, and his relationships to other people and objects, emotionally and spatially.

Any biological impairment which interferes with these experiences will distort the child's progressive interaction with his environment, and in turn distort the response of the social environment towards the child. The continuing interaction between an impaired child and his environment is thus at risk of becoming increasingly maladaptive. Impairments such as cerebral palsy (spasticity), which restrict *motor* development in a child, interfere with cognitive and language development too, because of the child's inability to explore the environment, and thus to conceptualize it. Additionally, the motor problems may affect the organs of speech, so the child's expressive language is blocked, unless some sign system is devised within the limits of the child's available movements. The inability to explore or express commonly leads to tremendous emotional frustration and behavioural difficulties. Even moderate degrees of spasticity may result in clumsiness, body image problems (that is, an inability to relate one's own body parts to each other in space), and difficulty with the skills of self-care and hygiene. Children damaged prenatally by the effects of Rhesus incompatability in their mother, are not always intellectually impaired, but commonly develop athetoid cerebral palsy (which renders most movements uncontrollable, including those involved in speech production), and also high-tone deafness. If such a child is also intellectually impaired, his slow learning will be additionally hampered by his motor and hearing limitations, which will also need to be catered for in his educational programme.

A child with the syndrome of Early Childhood Autism on the other hand, is likely to exhibit well-developed mobility and balance, but be quite unable to imitate movements (e.g. pedalling) until physically handled through the motions. His inability to mime is part of the major disability profoundly affecting communication and social development characteristic of the syndrome. The hypersensitivity to some colours and sounds, the stereotyped behaviour patterns and the high levels of anxiety and distress, all encourage those around him to make maladaptive responses to him, if appropriate advice is lacking. Not all such children are severely retarded intellectually, but for those who are, the social learning is even more difficult.

Down's Syndrome may have associated with it, among other things, disorders of the heart and joints, short sight, cataracts or catarrhal deafness. People with Down's Syndrome are intellectually impaired to a variable degree, and additional physical impairments to learning must be kept to a minimum. Most people with Down's Syndrome, however, have a highly developed social awareness, and can learn a great deal by mimicry; a method the autistic or spastic child cannot use, for different reasons. Associated physical disabilities may impair learning in less obvious ways.

> A Down's Syndrome baby with unusually poor muscle was unable to grasp and use toys, and could participate in little play. His parents interpreted this as profound mental retardation, and were tempted to abandon their efforts. They were encouraged to provide their son with the locomotor help he needed, by holding his hands round the toys which provided sounds, colours and movements, and supporting his body so that he could see and hear comfortably. Muscle tone improved later, but the child had not missed all his early experiences in the meantime, and his parents remained enthusiastic.

Families, from experience, are aware of a normal pattern of early child development, of predictable sequences of skills at roughly predictable ages. Disabilities which restrict particular areas of development, or global development, will distort the child's maturation and acquisition of skills and remove the parent's yardstick of "normality" by which they set their expectations of him, and themselves as parents. Toilet training may be permanently abandoned after protracted failure, although the problem may be one of developmental immaturity and their premature timing, or of faulty techniques; both of these require some specialist advice. Similarly, socially disabling behaviours may be left to develop unchecked where parents feel they are inevitable as part of the condition. Not only parents feel they are navigating in uncharted waters, but many professional people peripheral to the field of intellectual disability are expected to provide help, and they too are often limited in their experience of potential paths of learning and development in such children (Gath, 1978).

There is now an enormous body of professional and parental knowledge and experience covering all aspects of growing up and living with intellectual and multiple handicaps. The dissemination of it, among parents, practitioners, policy-makers and planners remains an immense need. Investment in a systematized programme of regularly updating knowledge and awareness of such, would enable the sharing of the human skill resources, which is a principal need of handicapped people.

During the past 20 years the fine gradations in normal infant development have become the subject of much study and popular interest. In the wealthy countries, where widespread malnutrition and infections are no longer the primary problems in child care, the identification of developmentally-delayed children, and their subsequent management, have become increasingly sophisticated. The specialized expensive style of some assessment practices renders them an irrelevant luxury to those parts of the third world where clean water and an adequate diet are still not available to all children. The priorities of provision to intellectually disabled people in poor countries are considered in Chapter 6.

Although the organization of the service delivery can vary, there is a need for all infants to undergo routine developmental screening at intervals from birth, by people trained to identify deviations from normal developmental progress, if all impaired children are to have their handicaps kept to a minimum. When doubt exists about a child's progress in any aspect, the first need of the child is for a global assessment which has a medical basis. It is essential to identify as early as possible any disorder which can damage the child's development. These include past impairments whose final level of resulting disability is still unpredictable (e.g. birth injury to the brain causing changing patterns of spasticity later); active disorders currently causing damage to the nervous system and other organs (e.g. infections, inborn errors of body chemistry, lead poisoning); and those conditions known to be commonly associated with later manifestations of problems (e.g. some types of epilepsy, Down's Syndrome).

"Assessment" is a popular term among those professionals on the periphery of the special services to the handicapped. However, without further qualifications the term is almost meaningless. In the field of child health, assessment of the many individual facets of a child's development is increasingly specialized, and the specialists involved are increasingly aware of their interrelated roles. Regretfully however, the nature of "assessments" required for intellectually disabled *adults* is nowhere near as purposefully identified; and requests for their "assessment" quite commonly remain very vague.

Assessment without subsequent remedial intervention is of no value to the child, and in addition is capable of having a detrimental effect on the parents. Assessment is a continuous experience which incorporates remedial management, and which must involve the parents with the professionals. It consists of the skilled examination of the various ways in which a child functions, followed by special treatment and teaching to enhance the child's further development, which is then subsequently re-examined in order to direct the next stages of treatment and teaching. Physiotherapy is concerned with the development of posture, of body mobility and awareness and control. It overlaps with occupational therapy, which is concerned with the development of fine manipulative skills and their wide range of uses. Both fields also overlap with speech therapy, concerned with the development of chewing, swallowing and speech mechanisms, and of course the development of language. These three remedial specialties, together with orthoptists (who provide remedial treatment to eye muscles), psychologists (concerned with learning and emotional difficulties) and teachers (who assemble the special educational prescription for the child), pool their knowledge, experience and imagination with those of the paediatrician, to provide a continuing remedial programme. The skills of the social worker are concurrently applied to emotional and social problems within the family unit. The desired outcome of the prolonged application of so many professional skills will be the physical and emotional growth and maturation of the child and his family, with the minimum possible of disabilities and handicaps developing for all of them.

How, where and by whom the assessment–remediation–assessment–remediation process is provided will depend on local circumstances. However, it is essential to study the ability of parents to use whatever service is planned, before implementing it. Problems of distance, transport, other family claims, cultural demands, can all leave a valuable service useless to some families who need it.

In aiming to give the maximum help possible to impaired children, it is essential that professionals and service planners perceive the needs in their correct priority. (1) The first priority is for the child to be acknowledged *as a child*, with all the needs and rights of all children. (2) If the child has physical or neuropsychiatric impairments, they require investigation and treatment. (3) If the child is in addition a very slow learner, that will have to be taken into account in his overall plan of management.

This recognition of the universal needs and rights of *all* children, including the multiply impaired, has been gaining strength over the past decade, and was given great emphasis by the UK Government's publication of a special report on child health, *Fit for the Future* (DHSS, 1976). It has received further Government recognition since then, with the affirmation by the Secretary of State for Health and Social Security in 1980 that hospitals are not places for children to grow up in. (Although the *childhood* needs of intellectually impaired *children* are now being recognized, the *adult* needs of intellectually impaired *adults* seem to defeat the public imagination at present).

In the first year of his life, a child's parents and other older people help him to acquire the early skills: eating, listening, paying attention, communicating, responding. During the second and subsequent years, the child begins to use, and increasingly needs, his peers to learn with, although the role of the adult of course remains essential.

The acquisition of the basic skills in a very impaired child is likely to be much slower, or more difficult than in an ordinary child, who acquires such skills of living from a mixture of demonstration, experimentation and imitation. The speed of the ordinary child's successes will partly depend on his level of exploratory drive ("inquisitiveness"), and the subsequent encouragement supplied both by the outcome, and the parents' expressed enthusiasm. The raising of ordinary young children makes great demands on parents, demands they are sometimes unprepared for, and an impaired child's needs will make even greater demands. The parents will need professional help in guiding their child's learning, plus resources of family time in which to do it. The process of teaching a young spastic child to feed, with his problem of reflex tongue thrust, may use up hours every day for that activity alone. Parents will learn the technique from a speech therapist, but the amount of adult time required in a small nuclear family to feed such a child can produce tremendous domestic pressures. Most families manage to supply the time and devotion to meet their child's special needs, but in some families limited human resources, and competing demands from other family members, make it impossible to meet this sustained demand from within the nuclear family alone. Those social agencies through which society itself undertakes the supportive role of the extended family, in providing help to such a situation must remember that the first priority is *to provide the child's nurturance in a family setting*. The child's own family has a need to be supported, not supplanted, by the solutions offered to their difficulties. The support may contain some sharing of the child's care, inside the home, perhaps inside an additional family home, or in an alternative family home, with the provision of remedial teaching outside home. The support will include sensitive recognition of the parents' feelings about needing to use help. The traditional solution to such family tragedies has of course been to deprive such children of family life altogether, with a degree of waste in human life and sadness (and probably money) beyond calculation. It has been well described already by Oswin (1978).

From the second year of life onwards, a child learns increasingly from its peers, starting from wary observation of each other, and progressing to cooperative play. It is among his own peers that the child will eventually mature and establish his adult status. The child with physical and intellectual impairments has the same need to learn from and set standards by its peers, and this need must be recognized in any provisions made for it. The child with reduced locomotor and manipulative skills will have difficulty sharing toys, play and exploration with other children. Hearing, speech and comprehension problems will reduce communications between them. Enabling the impaired child to be involved with his peers, without restricting the activities of those peers, takes imagination and sensitivity on the part of the responsible adults, but it can be done, and to the enrichment of all the children. Such peer group experience in the early years may be provided for the impaired child by the extended family, by play groups and nurseries, and by nursery classes in ordinary or special schools. The presence of ordinary peers to provide normal models of development is a fundamental requirement in growing up to understand how life is lived. Some children, nevertheless, have major disabilities which require specialized teaching before they can start to learn usefully from other children. These are conditions which interfere with social learning in particular: blindness, deafness, early childhood autism, the dysphasias. The aim is to enable the child eventually to engage and learn with other children as well as with adults. Such a child's needs may be met by initial intensive separate education, or by the provision of special remedial programmes within a less specialized group of children. The method should be dictated by the degree of disability present: a child emotionally paralysed with anxiety by the activities of children he does not comprehend will not benefit from them until he has acquired some skills with which to interact with other children. Once he can tolerate or even enjoy learning with other children, his environment must expand to permit them their essential place in his life.

The middle years of childhood

It is always useful to be reminded that the Latin origin of the word education means "to lead out". Education is an unending process which occurs in all settings; it is not the sole prerogative of teachers, any more than the provision of care is only that of parents and their substitutes. The satisfactory outcome of adequate physical and emotional nurturance, together with an imaginative educational programme, will be a child maturing into adulthood, who (a) has a sense of personal identity, a sense of belonging, and who has a good self image; (b) is able to identify and make choices, and exercise direction over his life; (c) is alert, curious, imaginative, stable, and flexible enough to tackle and solve problems. To achieve any or all of these goals, a child must acquire skills in the areas of locomotion and manipulation, communication, symbolic imagery, play and leisure, social interaction, self help, domestic and environmental activities, and all these skills are of course interdependent. Locomotor skills are necessary in self-care and communication, while communication and social skills are involved in the development of good self-image, and play is necessary to develop symbolic imagery and help communication.

The development of *self-esteem* in children with impairments, especially the slow learners, needs serious attention, which may mean special help to perplexed parents in particular. Neglect of a child's developing value and self-image especially as adolescence approaches, will reap avoidable harvests of human sadness and relationship difficulties in years to come.

The range and combinations of disabilities possible among intellectually impaired children are clearly enormous. Professional teaching skills and facilities will be needed to advance the very passive poorly motivated child who engages little with his environment; for the grossly overactive child with a very short attention span who stays with no activity long enough to learn from it; for the Down's child capable of imaginative play but frustrated by his speech difficulties; and for the inaccessible autistic child unable yet to make sense of any human activity, who has to be compelled out of obsessional routines into new experiences. The educational task looks overwhelming, but it can be done, and is being done, with varying degrees of success. In the United Kingdom, for the past decade even the most severely impaired child has had the statutory right to education by qualified teachers, and the first generation of this system are now leaving school. The specialist teachers now have a body of knowledge and experience which will be of immense value to very slow-learning adults, when eventually the professional and organizational changes occur which will impel such exchanges.

Children with impairments of all kinds are seen, then, to be in even more need of organized education than ordinary children, to be in need of prescriptive teaching by trained teachers. The curriculum will be designed to enable each child to continue learning about himself, about other people, and about his environment; and the programmes will have to take account of the child's spontaneous behaviours (and in some impaired children they form a limited repertoire). The social and emotional development of the child will be towards an acceptable level of tolerance towards stress without undue passivity; towards spontaneity without excess impulsivity; towards a capacity for self-assertion without dominance. Such healthy emotional adjustment is difficult to define, or even to agree about, but slow-learning adults are expected to be more saintly than the ordinary population. Antisocial behaviour in very slow-learning adults (even if performed in ignorance), except when it is a focus of patronizing amusement results in less tolerance and greater deprivation of rights than applies in the general public.

Intellectually impaired children have an unending need of social and emotional education, and this need will continue well into adult life. All children require guidance of this nature, of course, but the slow learner needs much more demonstration, and explanation and experience of the situations other children grasp for themselves, or pick up quickly from watching others. The practical training in self-help skills proceeds both at home and in school for all children. In the case of impaired children, whose areas of development, levels of motivation, and types of learning problem can vary so widely, it is of immeasurable importance that the parents and the school work as a team for the child. Quite commonly, there is a considerable discrepancy between the skills and achievements exhibited by the child in his school and in his home. In school the child may cooperate in toilet training, and attempt to dress, whilst at home he does neither. The domestic reasons may be insufficient expectations, unsatisfactory techniques or inadequate practice.

The point was made earlier that the overall nurturance of any child must be provided within a family setting, and that the family must be supported not supplanted by services.

The first few years in the life of an impaired child may not make excessive physical demands on the family, especially if he acquires mobility, the capacity to feed himself acceptably, and is cheerfully responsive. Such a child may show global but not profound developmental delay, and is represented by many children with Down's Syndrome. Such demands are comparable to those made on parents by the uninhibited inquisitive adventures of the toddler, but the stage will persist beyond the usual duration; the toddler activities will continue in a larger, stronger child, able to climb and manipulate with greater success. Nevertheless, most intellectually impaired children pass through this stage eventually; their interest in the environment and their motor development, are channelled into satisfying pursuits and skills by their parents and teachers, and progress is recognizable.

Severe problems in behaviour

While many intellectually impaired children of 10 years old are exploring life and learning how to learn with all the enthusiasm of an ordinary 5-year-old, some will still be grossly hampered by their major physical and cognitive impairments. It is important that parents and professionals continue to persist with the reduction of dribbling (and therefore halitosis), with the prevention of contractures, with the training of looking, listening, discrimination, and with the development of attention span. Although the child's speech may be nil, and his understanding of speech very limited, his carers must be enabled to appreciate how the contents of their speech can help the child enlarge his knowledge of his world. The importance of rich spoken language in ordinary child development is well recognized but for impaired children and adults, additionally handicapped by reduced experiences, understandable spoken language is perhaps even more important. The inability to reply on the part of the child or adult can of course lead to an eventual reciprocal silence on the part of the parent or helper, and gradually their content of talk deteriorates from rich "informative speech" to sparse "controlling speech" (for example, "Eat your dinner"; "Put that down!"). Parents and others need to be shown the positive gains made by their patient and sustained efforts over long periods of time, and for this reason some form of easy recording system is necessary, particularly for those children whose development is extremely slow.

Children between the ages of about 8–12 years old, who are severely intellectually impaired, but who are not disruptive, can be at risk from an unintentional, if very loving neglect. The intense early years of diagnosis and assessment are past, the anxieties reawakened by adolescence are yet to come, and domestic life may have settled into a reasonable coping routine, with a patient acceptance of the apparent inevitability of the child's disabilities. These years are of tremendous importance in the child's developing awareness of himself, and loving appreciation and acceptance of himself by his family and community are foundation stones of his personality and later development. Nevertheless, at this stage in life parents may start to leave the teaching of ordinary daily survival skills (cooking, road safety), entirely to the school, and to perceive *their* role as principally *carers*, responsible mainly for the comfort and eternal protection of their child. This situation is not surprising as the earlier crises have passed, possibly other children and certainly other domestic demands have presented themselves, and if the impaired child is himself undemanding in his behaviour, there may be little pressure for change. One may say in some instances that the child has been "warehoused" at home, at least in relation to continuing teaching needs. Marital breakdown is frequent in families with an impaired child; the remaining parent, usually the mother, may then be under such general domestic pressures that there is insufficient time, energy and emotion to do more than love and care for that child.

During the "junior school" years of a very slow-learning child, it is likely that the siblings will start to develop their own problems in relation to him, his local status, and his present and future role in their life. Sibling responses to the situation reflect very much the parental ones. The other children of parents who find the impairments and behaviours a problem, an embarrassment, a source of constant anxiety, find they have difficulty in bringing friends home, tend to play elsewhere; and experience a conflict of anger and guilt about their responsibilities towards him.

> One young and devoted mother of a 5-year-old boy with Down's Syndrome described her pride and relief that the 8-year-old brother had already started promising to take care of his little brother when he was grown up. Counselling was instituted urgently, with realistic suggestions of other varieties of care available to those adults who continued to need it.

Some families require a family therapy approach in the management of the behavioural changes and emotional adjustments referred to earlier.

In material terms, bringing up an intellectually impaired child in a nuclear family is usually more costly than ordinary child rearing. Delayed toilet training, clumsiness, a prolonged destructive phase, delayed independence all take their toll from clothing, furnishings, and sometimes parental employability. There is a wide range of *practical* needs likely in such an affected family: such things as assistance with laundry, the provision of napkins and plastic pants (which fit the wearer), a reliable baby sitter, bathing aids, help with transport. Such practical help of course will involve some money, but quite as important is the application of *imagination*. Where this is lacking schemes can be ill-thought out, and result in wasted resources. Parents must be enabled to rank their needs in order of *their* priorities; these sometimes surprise the professionals.

> A mother of a heavy, multiply-handicapped and epileptic child was feeling both desperate and hostile to professional helpers. She was angered at repeated recommendations to put her beloved child "in a home", to solve the problems she (and the professionals!) had with him. When asked what help she *did* want, she exploded "the bath"! Simple building alterations, with a bath aid, relieved her realistic fears of the child drowning during a fit in the bath, and improved her relationships with professionals whom she then perceived as listening to her needs.

It is during childhood that men and women start to develop concepts about their future identity and social roles. In a few children, a perceived role will provide strong motivation to prepare systematically for a vocation. A range of common roles will be expected by most children; to be a wage earner, to become a householder, to be independent, to have children, and certainly to be a member of the next generation of adults. The child whose disabilities leave him in prolonged dependence upon his parents, will be gravely handicapped in his preparation for adulthood, if no expectations or plans exist for him and his family after childhood is past.

In most western countries the social expectation is for young adults to leave the parental home by their mid-twenties, be it for marriage, study or otherwise and to live among people of their own age. It has however been a universal assumption that intellectually impaired young adults should remain at home with their parents for ever, or until a crisis occurs. Doubtless the patronizing view of intellectually impaired men and women as "perpetual children" encourages this assumption, but even the enthusiastic promotion of "community care" for slow learners seems to present the parental home as the central model of residential provision. That model means of course that an adult must remain a permanent guest in the home of the previous generation; there is no doubt as to whose home it is, and whose are the decisions in it.

During the childhood years, the presence of disabilities is likely to interfere with the child's various experiments in self-determination, and to leave undeveloped the parents' expectation of eventual adult status for their child. The expectation of an infinite parent-dependent child relationship is shared and promoted by most professional agencies. (It is of course much cheaper for society to have the special needs of these adult members supplied by their aging parents). However the tacit acceptance by society that the parent–child roles will be infinite, intrudes gravely into the personal development of both the impaired individual, and the parents. While one child will be at risk of underfunctioning, of being poorly motivated towards any self-determination, and indeed of learning to exploit the dependent role, another child will resent the restrictions of his situation, and show it in his behaviour. Hitherto, parents faced with an inevitable and eternal responsibility for their disabled offspring have accepted it with patience and commitment, and as a result many have remained emotionally and socially underdeveloped for the rest of their own lives. For intellectually impaired adults to live out their lives among their own generation in their neighbourhood, not only must the practical arrangements be planned, but *that expectation must be made explicit during that person's childhood*. For middle-aged and older parents, who have spent twenty or thirty devoted years supervising and caring for their offspring whom they have known to be dependent and vulnerable, it is exceedingly difficult to abandon that role and responsibility. Risk-taking will always have been kept to a minimum, and the anxiety provoked in such older parents by the proposed growth towards independence for their "children", can be quite unbearable, and risk-taking will be intolerable. Preparation by parents and children (impaired and intact) for eventual normal separation of the generations involves both practical and emotional aspects, which continue through childhood and adolescence. Future options for adult life must become apparent during the adolescence of impaired as well as intact people.

As with all children, attitudes towards life in general will be absorbed by the slow-learning child from his family. Is life presented as mostly a series of difficulties and risks to be avoided? Or is life to be lived adventurously? The disabled child risks being additionally handicapped if his parents have only anxious expectations for his life. The awareness of one's disability, differences, and vulnerability will inevitably bring anxiety, and disabled people need help in dealing with it, if they are not to be additionally handicapped by the effects of it. It is common for people who find most of life to be an anxiety-provoking affair, to arrange their lives with great regularity and strict routines to keep some control over the events they experience. Some people are temperamentally made that way, some are brought up so, and many respond that way when faculties diminish in old age and life becomes more confusing. Intellectually impaired people often develop rather rigid patterns of living for similar reasons: set routines present less challenge and effort, and reduce anxiety. Of course, routines are necessary to us all for survival, but so also is the capacity for new experiences. However, the anxiety some parents endure when imagining what life could do to their vulnerable disabled child, leads them to shelter the individual from risk-taking. Thus, he never learns to calculate risks, to deal with dangers nor how to tolerate anxiety. These aptitudes need to be developed from childhood onwards, and whilst teachers may be promoting them, parents are likely to be in need of a lot of help before they can do so too. Life is not a totally predictable affair, and all children should be enabled to grow up capable of living with some uncertainty. Those intellectually impaired children who grow up to live on "tramlines" of habit and are even encouraged to do so by their families' adherence to them, are at serious risk of major emotional disorder when an inevitable interruption of routine eventually occurs.

There is another mixed group of problems which can complicate intellectual impairment, and which needs special management. Children who have been damaged by encephalitis (inflammation of the brain substance) are subsequently particularly prone to become grossly and continuously overactive. The term "hyperkinetic" has been squandered and become discredited, but the combination of motor restlessness, need for little sleep, and very short attention span which together can persist for years in these intellectually impaired children, does perhaps deserve the term. With the reduction of childhood infections in the western world this behavioural sequel to some "brain damage" may be less common now: however, in parts of the United Kingdom where immigrant children are still at risk of tropical virus infections, there is the possibility of greater numbers of these children requiring extra facilities in their later management.

Although such gross overactivity, during the night as well as the day, can sometimes be improved by drugs, very commonly the children react very badly to medication, unless it is to control fits, and the principal method of management remains an educational one. This type of behaviour in a slow-learning child is utterly exhausting to parents, and needs skilled handling by the teacher. Until education was made statutory 10 years ago in the UK, these children were inevitably excluded from Junior Training Centres by staff ill-equipped to deal with such problems, and the families were left to contain their disruptive, destructive, agile children 24 hours a day. They were almost all admitted to long stay hospitals by their desperate parents.

Although the number of such children is fairly small, at least in the UK, the degree of disruption and despair each individual can create in his family, school and every other setting is enormous, and can last for years; the behaviour if unchecked becomes a well-rehearsed habit, and provides immense, even intractable problems in adult life. For these reasons, the needs of such children must receive the highest priority for professional skills, and staffing resources. Appropriate sustained intervention can commonly be expected to improve the situation by adolescence.

Daily life with a child who is so restless and unpredictable is extremely wearing, and parents need regular and frequent relief from the constant need to observe and occupy the child. In supplying the relief, the child's own need to continue learning in a domestic setting must not be denied, and the practical help must meet both types of need with the least disruption. Those adults providing parental relief must be familiarized with the family, the child, and his specific management programme. On no account must the child be caused to perceive himself as a burden, nor the parents to feel inadequate and expected to be grateful. Both do occur.

Social intercourse between adults and children, indeed between any people, involves influencing one another by communication and negotiation. The slow-learning child will have difficulty learning how to do both of these, and can be totally confused by the incomplete messages and muddled methods he encounters. Ordinary adults and older children convey a lot of communication by casual means, by nuances, incomplete sentences, and gestures which others usually understand. Misapprehension can, and of course often does, occur then, but total failure of comprehension and confusion develops in the very slow learner, if what is wanted from him is not made simple and explicit. It is not enough, either, to describe or demonstrate what behaviour is wanted from the child; the behaviour must be made to seem worthwhile by its results or its rewards. In the development of ordinary children, earlier rewards will include delighted parental reaction (for example father's excited encouragement of the spontane- ous babbling of "da–da"), and later rewards will include the satisfaction of completing a task (buttoning the last button, finishing the jigsaw). All children need an adult to help them use early opportunities for play, and capacity for self-direction in play develops over a long time. Adult interest and involvement in the child's activities will remain essential for much longer than usual in the intellectually impaired child.

It is very easy for communications between adults and a slow-learning child to become very distorted, if the adult's behaviour towards the child unwittingly conveys unintended messages. For example the restless mischief of all toddlers is demanding for the parent, and a few minutes when their child is self-absorbed and quiet is seized gratefully by the parent to attend to something else. It is when the child starts to bang and shout, that the parent again pays attention. The ordinary child however continues to increase his use of self-directed play; as his attention span lengthens, the activities bring rewards in themselves. The very slow-learning child however is at risk of remaining much longer in one stage of learning, so if he is as yet unable to occupy himself, he is likely to absorb with prolonged practice the lesson that when he is unoccupied, the quickest method to bring and hold the missing attention of an adult is to create some form of uproar. The attention may finally consist of exasperated shouts and smacks, but that form is better than none at all! The communications between the adult and child have become totally distorted; the adult responses have actually encouraged the child to communicate his needs in a highly unsatisfactory way.

It should be remembered, too, that children who still have a very short attention span seek constantly changing distractions. In the absence of other frequently varied activities, the very human activities displayed by exasperated and distraught parents and grandparents in response to "attention-seeking behaviour" can be full of changes: cajoling, shouting, sweeties and smacks! The child (not always intellectually impaired of course) who has learnt that disruptive ways of behaving guarantee social attention is, with his carers, in urgent need of help. The eventual outcome of such untreated disruptive behaviour will of course be exhausted, increasingly rejecting parents, with loss of family and neighbourly tolerance; and a child moving towards adulthood constantly practising the art of disruptive behaviour, while steadily absorbing the lesson of how unpleasant and unlovable the parents and others increasingly view him. To grow up learning that one is unlovable and unattractive is a most fearful lesson. The intellectually impaired person will not comprehend the origins, the implications, nor resolutions of their appalling predicament. The help necessary for such an individual and his parents and carers includes professional skills to examine and alter the ways the parents and child interact together, and counselling for the inevitable emotional difficulties present.

Adolescence

Before examining how adolescence can be experienced by very slow learners, it is useful to consider the hierarchy of human needs suggested by Maslow (1968). The most fundamental needs are the physiological ones, and they are followed by the need for protection against danger and deprivation, and the threat of them. There is next the group of social needs, that is the need to be with others, to be accepted by them, and to experience love and affection. There follow the ego needs for self-esteem, self-confidence, achievement, competence, the need for status and respect. Finally, there is a need for self-fulfilment, to fulfil one's potential for development. Because some people learn very slowly or with difficulty, it must never be assumed that the hierarchy of human needs does not apply to them; indeed it is the very failure to recognize and meet all these classes of need that has created so many problems for them and for others up till now. Adolescence brings major changes in body size and proportions, the child becomes taller, heavier, more muscular and changes facially. In the child who is still very dependent on bodily care, this brings added problems in bathing, dressing, toileting and mobility for his parents who are likely to be approaching middle age themselves. A great many handicapped young people are cared for by their mothers only, and the sheer physical effort demanded by stairs, wheelchairs and access to cars is exhausting. The application of appropriate equipment and extra pairs of hands at the right time are examples of the need to apply imagination to the situation. The increase in physical size also brings added difficulties if the child needs physical as well as verbal control over his activities; it is much more difficult to handle resistance in a lad of fifteen than in one aged seven. In that small number of adolescents whose relationships have been developing in a maladaptive direction the growing awareness of their physical strength may lead them to use it aggressively, to insist on getting their own way, and sadly this is most commonly directed at the mother. If this problem does start to develop, it needs to be intercepted with professional help promptly and early on. The advent of sexual maturity brings its own demands, and preparation for this should have been happening since infancy, in both disabled as well as intact children. Much knowledge about sexual behaviour and reproduction is disseminated by children and young people among themselves; the disabled child is almost guaranteed deprivation of information from this source as his disabled peers are likely to be less informed and to be less able to communicate what they do know; in addition the opportunities for private exchanges, such as while walking home from school, are missing from the lives of children who are escorted and supervised all the time. It is therefore of the utmost importance that the slow-learning child is taught about the sexual biology of men and women carefully and acurately.

At the same time the emotional and social aspects must be taught, although the real foundation lessons about warm supportive and caring relationships are taught from infancy by the conduct of parents towards one another, to all the children, to grandparents and neighbours. It is difficult to convey to an intellectually impaired young man at the peak of his sexual development the need to consider a woman's wishes, if at home he has never known his mother's (or anybody else's) feelings to be treated with courteous consideration. The nature of menstruation, ejaculation, masturbation, when and where they occur, their effects, their intimate nature, all need to be explained to both boys and girls. Only thus can they learn (and not necessarily very slowly) to be sensitive to the circumstances of one another. The nature of sexual relationships, intercourse, pregnancy, childbirth and contraception needs careful explanation, with quite as much attention to accuracy as is provided for ordinary children. The need for accurate understanding of sexual matters is of utmost importance to the future safety of intellectually impaired girls and boys. One obvious reason is to protect young women from sexual exploitation; however, the young men are in one sense at even greater long-term risk if they are sexually ill-informed; not only must they understand that they cannot impose their sexual wishes on others, but they must be taught very firmly the very strict views society and the law have about any sexual contact whatever with little girls and boys. Innocent inquisitiveness and naive willingness on the part of an intellectually impaired young man can lead to public and prolonged labelling of him locally as a sexual molester.

> A sixteen-year-old lad with a mental age of ten had received no sexual instruction in his somewhat disordered home. He was invited into the bushes to show his male anatomy to a ten-year-old girl, who provided him with the reciprocal information. Nothing further happened, but the girl went home and told her parents who then informed the police; the boy subsequently appeared in court and though no further action was taken he was then labelled locally for a long time as a sexual molester.

Parents who now are past middle-age very commonly found sexual instruction of all their children difficult. Ordinary children found things out for themselves but the many intellectually impaired adults now in their 30s and 40s have an inaccurate understanding of sexual matters, and sometimes lack the appropriate courtesies.

> During a parents' evening at an Adult Training Centre the elderly parents of a 35-year-old woman protested vehemently at the suggestion that slow learners needed as much sexual information as anybody else. They claimed their daughter had managed perfectly well without it and did not need her innocent life complicating by it. It was known however by the Centre's staff that the daughter in question was only too well aware of her own sexuality and had overwhelmed some of the lads with her enthusiastic advances. In denying the existence of her sexuality the parents had failed to provide any training in how to control and apply it.

Physical changes in their disabled child will reawaken anxieties in the parents: worries about what happens after leaving school, about how this changing adolescent will turn out, and most fearful of all, what will happen when the parents are no longer able to provide the necessary care. If the siblings are starting to leave home this anxiety is especially emphasized, while at the same time the physical help they may have provided is also diminishing. It is during adolescence that any unresolved interaction problems between the child and his parents or the child and his siblings come to a peak. The adolescent himself will be sensitive to the parental anxieties and to the fact that his status is somehow changing like his body. Changes will be happening in his social environment, siblings and friends will be growing up, becoming more independent, leaving home (and leaving him lonely), and older school friends will be leaving school. Change is imminent but the direction is usually undefined. The intellectually impaired youngster becomes more aware of his difference from other adolescents and his self-esteem is very vulnerable. Provided the young person has a basic repertoire of social skills with which to behave, however, such impaired adolescents are observed to transfer into the adult environment of the Training Centre or Work Preparation Centre with an almost audible sigh of relief at leaving the world of childhood behind. This change from childhood to adulthood is also noted by society at large, and social attitudes and prejudices change with it. While commonly there is public tolerance and pity for the "mentally handicapped" child, "mentally retarded" adults, especially men, present all sorts of threatening images to the general public, especially the older members of it. There are various common fantasies about intellectually impaired men, such as that they are potential sexual maniacs and that they are liable to be very violent. The public, of course, is at infinitely greater risk of sexual assault and violence from people of normal intelligence. However, the development of suspicion and unease towards intellectually impaired adults in the local community can obstruct the planning of facilities for them, and reduce the acceptance of slow-learning citizens in the world to which they have a right. It is human to be uncertain and cautious about unfamiliar behaviour, however, and the odd appearance or bizarre activities acquired by some intellectually impaired adults will make them appear deviant and frightening to strangers. It is therefore absolutely essential that very slow-learning children are groomed to pass into adult life free to the greatest extent possible from those aspects of behaviour and appearance which mark them out as different from "ordinary".

The kindly tolerance of odd behaviours and acceptance of inappropriate dress does a lifelong disservice to intellectually impaired adolescents and actually seriously *handicaps* them in their adult lifetime. Socially inappropriate behaviour, even if quite harmless, or even endearing, if it is allowed to persist will leave the intellectually impaired adult being patronized as a perpetual child and devalued in every way.

> Following a discussion in which this subject was explored, a clergyman who had tolerantly endured a painfully boisterous bear-hug every week after morning service from a lady with Down's Syndrome decided to offer her a warm but conventional hand-shake instead of a reciprocal bear-hug in future. The lady accepted the hand-shakes very readily; some weeks later, the clergyman realized that many more members of the congregation were now coming forward to shake hands with the lady concerned. Her hugs, harmless if embarrassing to others, were definitely harmful to the social development of the lady herself. This intellectually disabled person was *socially handicapped* by being tacitly encouraged to continue childish activities into adult life.

Adolescence, then, is the time in which the slow learner must have all areas of self help and survival skills reassessed and improved. The able-bodied adolescent who remains without responsibility for his hygiene, appearance and self-care, who is expected to make no contribution to the home in practical help, is entering adulthood with the enormous handicaps of being incompetent and being devalued. A situation commonly encountered is that of impaired adults capable of simple industrial assembly work and making the coffee in the Training Centre enrivonment, but unable to bath or shave themselves and unaware of when to change their socks or the bed linen. There is a tremendous need for parents and teachers to construct together programmes of *survival* training for these young people. Ordinary children have many opportunities to acquire survival skills and can learn about them from many sources. The slow-learning child will need to have explained not only *how* to do things, but *when* to do so, when *not* to do so; imagination needs to be applied with the help here too. Parents will set themselves fresh targets when confronted with a theoretical model of their intellectually impaired adolescent being left alone for 24 hours in their house: could he or she prepare a simple hot meal or drink safely? Could they keep warm, keep the doors locked, use the telephone, bath or wash safely? Clearly, the range of skills possible will vary according to the person's physical and intellectual difficulties, but most slow learners are not physically restricted nor profoundly retarded and are capable of learning to do most personal and domestic things appropriately; that is, if the lessons are carefully taught and regularly practiced.

> A very slow-learning boy of fifteen presented with protracted behavioural problems at home. They included gross overeating from the pantry, faecal soiling, and public scenes when he would lie on the pavement or scream in the car if thwarted. His behaviour was unexceptional in school. His adult height and weight made his management very difficult and the onset of physical aggression towards both parents prompted his admission to another domestic setting for assessment. It then became apparent that he had no idea of how to start washing or dressing himself nor how to clear a meal table. His self-image was abysmal and focused on his faecal functioning. The young man was started on various "Goal Plans" whereby he learnt to bath and dress himself, to participate domestically and he was given tremendous encouragement and praise. Control was kept on his diet, so his bowels functioned normally and he became thinner and very attractive. His self-esteem rose visibly and he moved into more adult circles. The family dynamics behind his maladaptive development were complex but the ego needs of the young man to develop competence and self-esteem could be met by practical help.

The young person with additional physical impairments who is restricted to a wheelchair, who cannot share in the practical, personal and domestic tasks will have yet greater difficulties in finding an adult role and in meeting the ego needs for self-esteem and competence. The problems of preserving human dignity and individuality while providing the most intimate of care to any very disabled person are enormous. Not surprisingly, some highly dependent young people develop into demanding and difficult ones; and yet many such gravely disabled youngsters are to be found sharing family life as the focus of love and good humour and giving a great deal by their personalities. There is still everything to be learned about what disability can give to

life as well as take from it. The multiply-disabled adolescent, then, has
more problems than most, and yet this person gets the least help. In
Britain for example, it is likely that, during childhood, paediatric,
educational and welfare provision will be available to meet the mixed
needs until about sixteen years old. After that, the young multiply-disabled person and his family are likely to drop over a metaphorical cliff
of services because at the end of childhood the coordination of
physical, educational and welfare care stops. The impact of this second
variation of bereavement on the young person and his parents can
result in chronic depression and hopelessness. The numbers of such
multiply-disabled young people are not large and could be catered for
given the local political will. In Britain at least, provision of education
for the severely disabled child is compulsory until he is 16 years old,
but subsequent education and training are not, and they are dependent
on local political priorities. As a result, at the time of major uncertainty
for the slow-learning adolescent and his family, the security of school
ends, without guarantees of subsequent education to follow, or indeed
guarantees of any substantial help in the future. The greater the need
for physical help the less likely is it to be available.

Intellectually impaired adolescents approach adulthood with a wide
variety of strengths and needs. Physically they may be of unremarka-
ble appearance or be retarded in growth also; they may be spastic or
have the features of Down's Syndrome. Associated with all varieties
of appearance there can be any level of achievements, so that a young
man of ordinary appearance may have developed few skills of self-care
or concentration, while a person who has Down's Syndrome may be
capable of living independently. The type of training to be continued
through adolescence into adult life must be dictated by the stage of
development reached. The cessation of full-time education at about
16-years-old, when most slow learners have the mental age and
enthusiasm of a 5- to 7-year-old learner, is a great waste. There is a
tremendous need to continue the education, yet at the same time to
ensure that the young person fully becomes an adult. This need is very
obvious in, for example, a young person with Down's Syndrome who
is beginning to read and write and handle money at the point of leaving
school. However, the need to continue with prescriptive teaching is
perhaps even greater in the profoundly-impaired adolescent with a
short attention span, who has not yet learnt to sit for long and enjoy
any sustained activity, those who are bored and endlessly seeking
human attention. It is for these young adults with their unmet needs
for continuous treatment and teaching that institutional care is
commonly sought eventually in desperation. The acquisition of a

range of leisure skills shared by ordinary local adults, besides providing intrinsic enjoyment, will provide new acquaintances, greater acceptance and so further opportunities to learn from ordinary people how to live life. It is a great advantage to a young man to have learned how to kick a football around accurately, to play snooker or to fish. Equally characteristic leisure activities are perhaps less identifiable among girls, but would certainly include dancing and swimming. Severe physical disability does not always have to prevent the practice of such leisure pursuits, as many physically disabled people can demonstrate. For such youngsters to experience and practice these leisure activities does mean that parents, instructors, friends or volunteers need to be available and capable of helping them, and that transport is available to get there. Lack of suitable transport is a common obstacle to a great many available leisure activities.

Adolescence, then, is the period of life in which intellectually impaired people must be preparing, with their families, for adult status, for adult facilities, for the continuous acquisition of adult skills, and for the development of mature emotional interdependence with other people.

The Needs of Intellectually Impaired Adults

At eighteen years of age, in Britain all adolescents achieve legal adult status, even those with serious disabilities. Except in the occasional situation where an adult is subject to a Guardianship Order or similar imposed legal restraint, nobody is in a position to give or withhold "consent" to lawful activities of an intellectually impaired adult. Parents for example are not entitled to give or withhold "consent" for such an adult to go swimming or on holiday, nor can Local Authorities "permit" or "refuse" the discharge of an adult to other accommodation, unless the law has been invoked to impose that degree of control. Some parents and some professionals need regular reminding as to whose opinions and wishes hold priority. Common sense dictates that for much of the time parents and carers will share in the decision-making; nevertheless, it is of fundamental importance that from childhood onwards intellectually impaired people are helped to practice making choices, taking decisions, and examining the outcome of those decisions. Needless to say, if they are to trust the advice and guidance they receive in doing this, it must always be of the utmost integrity. It is observably difficult for some older parents to envisage the wide range of available choices to be practised in everyday life by impaired adults. It may reflect pressures which militated against conscious decision-making during the parents' own lives. Choice in such matters as clothing, bedtimes, diet, relationships, may be permitted or denied to people whom the law has not deprived of such a right. It can occur at home as well as in institutions, and demonstrates society's failure to recognize the needs for self-esteem and respect of its very slow learners. All individuals need stimulation and a constant supply of new experiences if they are to continue personal development. The increases in abilities and knowledge from these experiences enable an individual to change his relationship to his environment and so gain better control over it and himself.

Intellectually impaired young adults then must therefore continue with formal instruction in all areas of self-help and survival skills, using whatever technical aids and adaptations are necessary; using every life event as a learning experience, and using all resources to improve communication skills. Their social life must be extended into that of ordinary local adults, particularly those of their own age. Intellectually impaired adults do *not* need patronage or indulgence, but courteous and discreet guidance about customary adult conduct. Where the individual suffers from limited or no speech, there is an extra need to avoid the dehumanizing practice of talking above them, as if they were not present.

Adults in long-stay hospitals

It is during early adult life that the final choice of ultimate life style for an intellectually impaired adult has often been made. There are a great many adults with profound learning difficulties since childhood, who never received the intensive, sustained individual prescriptive teaching that they needed, and whose resulting behavioural difficulties in childhood, adolescence or early adult life developed beyond the management of their families. They were admitted finally as in-patients of large hospitals which contained only intellectually impaired people as co-residents. Sometimes the reason for admission was not difficult behaviour, but simply physical dependence on other people for toiletting, dressing and feeding, when parents could no longer do it. When the needs of one very impaired person have become greater than two parents can meet, society has arranged for the needs of some thirty or more similar people to be met by about four nurses. The greater the intellectual difficulties, the communication and sensory impairments, or the locomotor disabilities, the less has been the investment of skills and professional interest in these people, and the more impoverished has been their environment. It is such men and women who remain on the back wards of "mental handicap" hospitals, who still miss out on individual programmes of training, and who are only ever treated as part of a cohort. They are required to live corporately, though many of them will still be at a developmental level of 12–24 months, so they will not be ready to learn much from, or even interact with, one another. The profiles of achievements and social behaviours of such people who are compelled to live together, are likely to vary widely, and any one of the men and women in that situation will proceed into middle-age and beyond surrounded at all times by the incontinence, noise and aggression of other people, in bleak shabby surroundings. It is not surprising that some individuals come to learn (for they are still learners), that to smash a window, bite somebody or hit one's head on the wall will bring some brief highlight of attention and personal interaction, even if painful. It is with such very intellectually impaired adults, who have rehearsed their maladaptive behaviours uninterruptedly for years, surrounded only by people who behave in as equally useless a fashion, that the fundamental philosophy of a society and its agents towards slow learners is really put to the test.

Men and women whose lives are spent without comfort, privacy, beauty or dignity, are not likely to recognize or appreciate such qualities to the full, on a first encounter. Many such adults have had their behavioural disorder neglected for so long, that to ameliorate it requires an investment of skill and staffing of an order more usual to an Intensive Care Unit. This is a useful comparison; it begs the question of why intensive psychological treatment does not seem to have the same priority as intensive physiological treatment. If all humans are valued as humans, then all treatment needs must be evaluated on that basis.

The damage done to intellectually disabled people, firstly by the failure to respond to their specific impairments, and secondly by the deprivation in their "treatment" environment, accumulates as an added handicap to their primary impairments. Their lack of practice in ordinary living is comparable to the fixed contractures which occur in spastic children and adults who have continued to grow, but without any practice in movements. Spastic children who have had regular physiotherapy however, although very disabled, are not as fixed; they are enabled to perceive the world from an upright position, and have the experiences of life literally brought within their hands.

The effects of failure to identify and meet the various needs of a growing person with impairments to learning can be represented diagrammatically, as shown in Figure 1. The impairments present at birth may be considered the *primary level of problems*. As the child grows, if the interaction with the environment and the learning are grossly distorted and maladaptive, the child acquires the secondary level of problems; for example, the deaf child unaided will not learn to speak, the slow child untaught will learn to be dependent, the frustrated child will become aggressive. Society's solution to the secondary level of problems in the past has been institutionalization, which by its removal of all ordinary social lessons from the person's life, has imposed the tertiary level of problems. The resulting collection of human beings, devoid of status, personal esteem, social

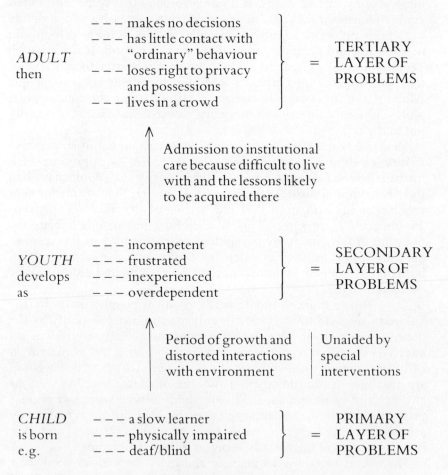

Figure 1. A hierarchy of problems for intellectually impaired people.

graces or experience are then perceived by planners and policy makers, as the corporate identity of "mental handicap". They are not. They are the end products of *failed* "mental handicap" care.

Not all the adults who live in big hospitals are profoundly impaired. It is estimated that in Britain some 15 000 people who are independent for self-care and free of behavioural problems, still live in big institutions simply because there are no ordinary dwellings available to them. The reasons for their original admissions are often unclear, and now irrelevant. Such men and women are not usually restricted to the same four walls every day, but they are often subject to the wearing of communal clothing, of sharing public ablutions and have no control over their lives. The personal appearance of such long-stay residents usually indicates the absence of full-length mirrors in their living quarters, and clothing chosen primarily to suit the laundry, not personal taste.

> A 32-year-old man had spent 12 years in a rather isolated all-male institution. On transfer to a rehabilitation setting, attention was paid to his very careless appearance. It became apparent that although he could identify others on film, and in a mirror image, he had no such recognition of himself. Although he has made rapid gains in other skills including vocabulary, it remains to be seen how much self-awareness he develops.

> A group of children who had spent several years in a big hospital, when visiting an ordinary home could only identify rooms in it as dayroom, dormitory and sluice. Domestic terms were not part of their experience, nor were their own clothes and toys.

Bereavement

Anxiety, vulnerability, loneliness, grief and pain are part of living, and although some individuals learn to submerge them under their life style, such experiences remain potentially ever present. Intellectually impaired people are especially exposed to such states; they *are* vulnerable, slow to understand, receive less explanation and have difficulty expressing their feelings of fear, anger and bewilderment.

It is only recently that recognition has been made of the bereavements experienced by so many slow learners (Oswin, 1981). The significance of the loss is often enormous: the grief is not only over a loved parent's death, but the associated loss of home, life style and all the ordinary familiar contacts if residential admission follows. For many such impaired people, the death has been left unexplained by well-meaning relatives, so that the disappearance of the parent is unaccounted for. Instead of the individual soon "forgetting all about it", their bewilderment, fear and distress mounts to unmanageable levels.

> The widowed mother of a pleasant 15-year-old boy with Down's Syndrome died suddenly. As he had always lived with her, he was admitted to a children's home. Within a week he started swearing, stripping, exposing himself and being aggressive. When urgent hospital admission was sought for this "aggressive mongol", it became apparent that nobody had explained where mother was, why the boy was in the home, nor explored his understanding of death. His need for some counselling sessions and the recognition of his state of mourning had been totally overlooked because he was "a mongol".

Death in western societies has become an unfamiliar experience; explaining and discussing feelings about it are difficult and unpractised. Ordinary children may have the practical and emotional experiences related to handling and burying small pets, but intellectually impaired children and adults may never have known even that. Mourning is part of the human condition, and very slow learners are not excluded from sharing it fully. They need the opportunity to explore the meaning of death via human rituals, and through the honest sharing of others' understanding of it. It is necessary for staff caring for such grieving individuals to recognize that moodiness, irritability, apathy are all part of mourning, and that grief heals very slowly. It can be very difficult for young members of staff who have never experienced a close bereavement to be empathic to this human state.

The human dimension of grief is unrelated to cleverness; so also is the life of the spirit. Not long ago the sexual experience of intellectually impaired people was an embarrassing subject and taboo. That is now changing, but death and bereavement remain a difficult subject. A spiritual dimension of life remains embarrassing and commonly taboo also. Mystics through the ages have described their similar numinous experiences, but language is still inadequate to the task. The intellectually impaired always experience inadequate language too, but attempts can be made to share with honesty one's understanding of love, integrity, human worth and personal experiences of a divine spirit.

Personal growth exists in more dimensions than just success and failure, and slow-learning people often illumine them in their lives.

A place to live

Whatever form home life takes, one's home is expected to provide comfort, privacy and security. During childhood the decisions about diet, furnishings, activities, the daily rhythms, are made by parents; adolescents can expect to make some of the choices themselves, and for adults the decisions about life style, activities and companions are no longer the responsibility of their parents. Because of their developmental delay, children who are physically disabled or intellectually impaired may have their practice in making choices left dormant, and their parents may overlook the need to develop active decision-making by their children and indeed by themselves. It is not yet customary for support services to advocate the examination of possible choices by intellectually impaired adults as well as their families.

Ordinarily, adults do their own homemaking. Those who, to whatever degree, are unable to do this, need somebody else to do this for them. This does not automatically mean being a guest in another homemaker's home. Traditionally people who lack the physical agility or skills to make a home for themselves, are accommodated residentially in a style and setting about which they have had no choice made available. The choice has customarily been taken by the person's parents, and the choices available have been either to remain under the parental roof—or to become a member of a residential community. This usually consists of hundreds of other disabled and unskilled residents, whose choices and decisions are made for them by people employed by society to do so. The tertiary layer of problems which have accumulated for the intellectually impaired person over the decades, from this method of meeting simple human needs, has already been described.

Intellectually impaired adults have a need and a right to choose their home life from a selection of options they have initially explored. Whatever is their choice, a varying amount of regular training and support will be required to achieve and develop their home life. The organization of such provision in their own locality will demand flexibility, and again imagination, in bringing together a practical recipe of local ingredients using statutory, voluntary and family resources. The variety of homelife to be made available will include the parental home, supported lodgings in another family home, a house shared with friends and supported by full-time or part-time residential homemaking staff, or a similar shared house with visiting staff support. The provision of home life starts with the supply of an ordinary dwelling in an ordinary neighbourhood, with the addition of ordinary adaptations necessary to help anyone with physical disabilities.

The role of a homemaker serving those adults permanently or temporarily unable to carry out that task for themselves, is one demanding far greater sensitivity than has been accorded it in the past. It starts with the continuous recognition of whose home it is; it belongs to the residents, and not to the support staff nor to their "department". The staff are there *to serve* the residents, as part of the residential facet of services to intellectually impaired people. The tasks required of the supporting homemakers will vary widely, according to the prevailing levels of disability and other available support. Like everyone else, intellectually impaired people are developing human beings. During the course of one person's lifetime the level of help needed will naturally change, for example training needs in early adulthood may be expected to have diminished by middle age, but the advent of old age may raise the level of need for other support again. The support to be provided in the home may include very intimate tasks concerned with bodily functions demanding sensitive attention to privacy and dignity; it will include the full use of every possible learning opportunity for residents to acquire competence in daily living; it will require the staff's capacity to reduce its influence as residents learn to take calculated risks in decision making.

The homemakers will contribute to a home environment which is of the residents' choosing; they will teach skills to the residents, and assist emotional maturation; they will ensure ordinary human encounters with neighbours, shop-keepers and public services, facilitate leisure and social pursuits in the locality; and they will collaborate with other professional contributors to the residents' care. Such homemakers will have a tremendous need for their own sustained professional support system and training, which must be of a very high quality. The monitoring of the service provided will need to be accorded much greater status than has been recognized to date.

The amount of input required from homemakers will depend on the resources already present among residents. The small group of people with whom an intellectually impaired adult chooses to live may be friends with whom he has grown up, or may contain other adults who have a need to share a home, such as people without families, or students. The satisfactory composition of a group choosing to share a home together will depend on several things. Initially, it will need the opportunities for a wide range of candidates to meet regularly in order to identify their mutual needs, strengths and compatibilities in both skills and personalities. It can help selection if a potential group is enabled to practice daily routines together in a training setting. The level and variety of outside support needed to run the home will become apparent, according to the skills and compatibilities present. The emotional and practical support which intellectually impaired friends can be seen to share with one another, has never been honoured as the tremendous resource it is. The pleasure in regular routines, and the pride in humble successes which many slow learners display are qualities which can contribute to the stability of home life for intact as well as impaired members of it.

During an adult's lifetime the nature of home life changes. The number of residents expands and contracts with the need for space changing accordingly. The emotional and social needs of members will change too. Intellectually impaired adults also face possible domestic changes; they may wish to move into other accommodation alone, with a friend, or to marry. Support staff will then be required to help them work our their needs, and the solutions possible. Where a married couple cannot manage in their own home even with visiting support, it is possible for them to live within the shelter of a larger group. Such a couple will need informed counselling on the desirability of having children and contraception.

Earlier in the chapter, reference was made to the problems of the chronically disruptive intellectually impaired adult. In any one locality they form a very small number, and individual treatment of their problems in their own accommodation by skilled staff has a greater chance of success, perhaps, than the usual collective containment of many behavioural problems in an environment almost totally unrelated to ordinary living.

Transition in lifestyle from living as a slow-learning adolescent with parents, to living as a householder with the degree of help necessary to do so, requires prolonged practice at many skills and increasing practice in emotional separation. Local facilities are needed to enable intellectually impaired young people to spend increasing lengths of time in alternative domestic settings from their parents home. The visits may start as a single meal and become extended to a week or more over time. It is likely that many co-residents experiencing such short-term care will already be well known to one another as colleagues in the local sphere of daily training.

The continuation of training and education in adult life

Intellectually impaired people of all ages are capable of acquiring new skills and abilities provided systematic and structured teaching is supplied. Intellectually impaired people usually have tremendous problems with learning spontaneously and in grasping situations. Such people have difficulty in transferring learned experiences from one situation to another. They do not easily "just pick things up". Even in a stimulating environment, progress is unlikely to be great if the objectives and teachings are not deliberately structured to meet that individual's requirements. The needs of intellectually impaired adults will vary according to the individuals, of course, but they must always include personal respect, the recognition that the needs will change during a lifetime and that an imaginative range of optional ways must exist to meet those needs. In addition to the necessity for a continuing structured educational approach to the provisions for slow-learning adults, there is another ordinary human need to be met, and that is of a regular change of environment. People who are very dependent on others may be at risk of spending every day of their lives within the same four walls, with the stultifying effects of such deprivation of stimuli. Part of the responsibility of ordinary adult status is to contribute in some form or other to the socio-economic life of the community, and intellectually impaired adults have a right and a need to contribute also with useful occupation or employment.

The needs for a social environment beyond home, for structured training in self-sufficiency, for personal care and "survival skills" and preparation for useful occupation or employment, will demand the provision of assessment and training facilities, for use daily by local adults who are of all levels of intellectual impairment. Physical and sensory disabilities which may also be present, will of course have to be catered for as another variety of need.

The range of needs to be met, and their fluctuations over time, mean that the relationship between the slow-learning adult and the daily occupation or training centre will have to be a dynamic not a passive one, with greater aims than keeping the individual "occupied". There are so many threads of development and progress in the lives of slow learners to be maintained and coordinated, in the home life, work and leisure spheres. Many individuals can be shown to have uneven profiles of achievement and adjustment over these three areas, especially if no formal coordination or overall life-plan has been arranged. So often, opportunities to transfer lessons to different situations in life (for example the use of numbers) are wasted because the relatives and instructors do not know what is happening in the other parts of the slow learner's life.

Employment or a useful occupation is of enormous importance to many intellectually impaired people. To be respected as a working adult gives to many a great sense of achievement and worth which is otherwise unobtainable. It has been demonstrated that many impaired people are capable of being trained for a variety of jobs provided the training is properly designed, and provided the trainee is also prepared for employment by the development of appropriate social skills, a work discipline and a capacity for sustained effort. The supervision of such an employee needs planning by the employer and the professional supporters. The variety of work situations can range from groups of employees working under supervision in horticulture or in factories, to individuals working in a service capacity in hotels and nursing homes. Sheltered employment may be more appropriate to many intellectually impaired people who can eventually maintain a reasonable work level given the necessary facilities, careful training and support.

High levels of unemployment together with inflexible local attitudes towards sexual roles can be very handicapping to intellectually impaired men.

> A strong man whose considerable learning difficulties were complicated by poorly controlled epilepsy and hot temper, passionately but quite unrealistically wanted to work in the heavy industry which employed his father and brothers. He was regularly teased by his insensitive brothers who had clear views of what was "men's work" and what wasn't. The client, of course, initially found training in domestic self-sufficiency quite contemptible as "women's work". His very aggressive outbursts after perceived offences to his sensitive pride made solutions to his needs even more difficult to supply.

Intellectually impaired young women have in the past been rather more readily occupied alongside their mothers in the home, but the young men have not been able to stay constantly at the side of their fathers who were at work. Young men create the most conspicuous peak of admission to permanent residential care. With the passing of the generation of older mothers who remained at home and the current changes in social expectations of employment for mothers and fathers, the modelling of sexual roles may become less distinct for slow learners, which may or may not be helpful to them.

Health needs

Intellectually impaired adults who are free from physical disability have the same need for ordinary medical care as anyone else. Unfortunately, they are at risk of receiving poorer quality health care, partly because of their frequent problems of communication, which can sometimes leave medical practitioners feeling inadequate and incompetent. Relatives and staff very familiar with the individual are usually sensitive to the existence of illness or disorder even if they cannot define it. A painstaking medical history from them, gentle patient physical examination, conducted with explanation and preparation, is possible in almost every clinical situation. Most special investigations are tolerated, again provided gentle slow explanation is given to reduce anxiety. Intellectually impaired people are even more readily frightened by pain, strangers, physical interference and raised voices, than intact people. The condition of Down's Syndrome sometimes seems to frighten doctors.

> A consultant psychiatrist was asked by a family doctor to see a "mongol" at home as she was said to be too difficult to assess clinically. The mother had reported that her daughter had acute abdominal pain. The young woman turned out to be very capable of answering for herself all the specific questions necessary, and then fully cooperated in the physical examination. Happily, there was nothing seriously wrong.

> A young boy with Down's Syndrome was brought by his father to the same psychiatrist in desperation, with inflammation and swelling of the foreskin. The child was in pain, terrified, and had fought off attempts to apply a prescribed ointment. A prolonged soak in the bath, with some plastic ducks and quiet chat, followed by application of anaesthetic jelly removed the pain and panic and cleared the way for a trauma-free circumcision a few days later. The label of "mongolism" had somehow interfered with the application of common sense as well as anaesthetic to his troubles for over two years.

The skills of dentists, opticians, chiropodists and audiometricians are all needed by slow learners at some time or other. The only extra ingredients needed are patience, courtesy, and careful, simple explanations in advance. These ingredients may occasionally have to be supplied on behalf of the professional by the client's companion; busy practitioners, in rare instances, have been taken aback in having to wait while introductions are explained, and permission is sought for bodily examination.

Psychiatric problems afflict intellectually impaired people more than the rest of the population; considering the stress, confusion, vulnerability and disparagement they have to cope with it is hardly surprising, and the presence of undefined organic brain damage has an unmeasured effect on mood, emotions and thought processes. Anxiety states, severe depression and obsessional behaviour are quite common, and states of hypomanic overactivity are well recognized, although normally lacking any euphoric component. A pragmatic approach combining the application of drugs, sensitive environmental manipulation and training to deal better with stresses can usually relieve the distress of the individual and his family significantly. In less impaired people with a reasonable vocabulary, the thought disorder of schizophrenia may be recognizable. However, such a diagnosis in a person without speech is little more than guesswork, although the distress present may demand empirical treatment as such.

> A young man (who also happened to have Down's Syndrome) was referred by his Training Centre manager for advice regarding the recent onset of bizarre behaviour. This included swearing, aggression, stripping and self-induced vomiting. The man had infected, chewed fingernails, was not eating, had lost weight; his family described loss of sleep, loss of interest and weeping. The man was of a rather obsessional personality who liked his life in rigid routines and loved domestic work. In the Training Centre, he had been rotated out of the domestic unit for more work experience, and he had become anxious and then depressed when his routines were interrupted. His family had lovingly reinforced his obsessional lifestyle. The clinical picture was one of severe depression and anxiety, and he responded rapidly to antidepressant drugs. This was followed up with programmes to widen his range of experiences and reduce his obsessional activities at home and at work.

It is to be hoped in future that the adequate surveillance of very slow learners from childhood onwards would identify the early stages of such maladaptive development and so help to prevent some varieties of mental ill health.

Later Life of Intellectually Impaired People

It is only during the past decade in western countries that such an aspect of the human condition has emerged. Previously, organic disorders commonly associated with severe impairment such as chest infections in people with Down's Syndrome or cerebral palsy, reduced life expectancy significantly. Successful efforts are made nowadays to reduce the level of organic disorders, by prevention and treatment with physiotherapy, drugs and other methods. As a result their life expectancy is now nearer to that of the general population. Very elderly intellectually impaired people are rarely seen at present outside of institutions, but people in their sixties are still living at home with aged parents, siblings or nieces. The domestic scene is sometimes rather sad, with an aged mother and late-middle-aged "child", quite unable to separate now, yet both having experienced a very restricted life.

In many large British institutions, the number of intellectually impaired men and women over the age of 75 in increasing rapidly, and the accumulating physical frailties of extreme old age require additional help. The original degree of intellectual impairment in the majority of these people is very questionable however; the reason for admission to an institution in their youth was sometimes no more than sexual promiscuity if a woman was also educationally (not necessarily intellectually!) retarded. The physical health of these elderly people is well maintained, and many are surviving into their nineties.

Little is known about the nature of old age as experienced by seriously intellectually impaired adults; it has not yet been studied. Down's Syndrome is well recognized as a condition associated with the early onset of ageing processes. However, there is a great need for systematic study of the effects of ageing on various physical and particularly psychological functions in people with different forms of intellectual impairment. In the western nations they, with all other adults, will one day be part of a very expanded elderly population; their expected strengths and needs must be included in planning, but at present we do not know if they are particularly special.

As men and women with advancing age are less able to contend with current demands, they draw increasingly on their reserve of memories of times past. The bleak poverty of experiences to remember, in the lives of thousands of elderly people after decades in institutions, is quite painful to contemplate. The lives of those who have remained at home may have contained more variety but it is not always certain. Until now the lives of elderly intellectually disabled people have passed from a prolonged childhood into incomplete adulthood, which simply merged into old age. For them there will have been no recognizable "Seasons of a Man's Life".

In this chapter, an endeavour has been made to set out as clearly as possible the nature, variety and extent of the needs which must be met if (a) intellectual or multiple impairment is to be minimally disabling, having regard to its original severity; (b) impaired children and adults are not to be unnecessarily handicapped, materially or socially, as a result of their disabilities; (c) parents, brothers and sisters, and others close to the person with the impairment, are to be enabled to understand, to assist, to train, educate and care—without themselves being deprived of a full life.

All these needs can only be met if the society of which the intellectually impaired child or adult is a *member* has been brought to a stage in its own evolution where a communal responsibility is fully accepted, and where that membership is recognized. Different societies within the "Old World" and the "New World" still differ significantly in terms of such a development. Those in the "Third World" are in most cases still struggling with the enormous problems of poverty, malnutrition, endemic disease—and cultural change enforced and accelerated by economic and political pressures. In the next chapter, we look at just some of the different ways in which the countries of the "Old" and "New" worlds have mobilized their traditions and their resources, to fashion structures of service both voluntary and public, the object of which is to meet the needs of a numerically tiny proportion of their numbers, until very recently a silent majority.

CHAPTER 3

Structural Models of Service Delivery

The nature and extent of services provided to intellectually disabled people and their parents or relatives are obviously unlikely to be independent of the national, regional and local philosophies, priorities and structures existing in their country of residence. While no attempt will be made here to provide a comprehensive international coverage, it does seem essential to provide examples of some of the main structural models. One large group combining similarities with variety is to be found in countries with a federal political structure, such as Canada, the USA and Australia. In all these countries, the similarity lies in the sharing of service responsibilities between federal government, state (or provincial) government, and voluntary (or "non-profit-making") bodies. The variety is to be found in the ways in which this sharing is organized and financed. The second group comprises the geographically smaller non-federal countries, of which Eire, New Zealand and the Nordic group are examples. A third model is provided by the United Kingdom, where a national health service has held the primary responsibility involving an interface at city or county level with the educational and social services of local government, and leaving a relatively minor service-providing role for the voluntary sector.

These three structural models which will now be described are of course not wholly independent of one another; overlap is naturally considerable. However, their use does provide a basic framework within which to consider the ways in which needs are—and are not—met by the service-providing agents.

Large Federal Countries

The USA

Services for the intellectually disabled person in the United States of America are greatly affected by Federal Government initiatives and

48

In all Australian states there are examples of three types of residential provision (in addition to the family home). There are state health commission hospitals; nursing homes operated by voluntary non-profit organizations or by private enterprise; and hostels or other small-scale residential units, most of which are operated by voluntary bodies. One state, Western Australia, has succeeded in completely removing all intellectually impaired people from the mental hospitals, and the state's largest unit contains 36 beds in an overall provision of 160 for a known population of 6000 persons. All remaining accommodation is in the family home or in units located in ordinary suburban streets, with the architecture of the premises designed to fit in with neighbouring dwellings. Since 1976, the state of Queensland has been implementing a policy designed to achieve a similar outcome and eventually to surpass it in ways that will be described later in this volume. Western Australia was until recently unique in offering a career course for residential care which is *not* based on a "nursing model". It has now been joined in this by Queensland. Both states were able to take advantage of the absence of specialist nursing qualifications in "mental retardation" nursing; when Queensland introduced its new philosophy in 1976, the nurses in the state institutions for the mentally retarded were simply "moved sideways" to augment the trained staff in the psychiatric hospitals. Two other states, Victoria and Tasmania, are currently endeavouring to implement the recommendations of major official reports (1977, 1980) both of which aim at patterns of community living with appropriate supportive services.

The role and organization of the voluntary non-profit-making sector also varies widely from state to state, ranging from large numbers of relatively small bodies to the single large organization in Queensland which operates 25 schools, 39 homes and hostels, 20 workshop/activity centres, 5 farms and 4 clinics. Voluntary bodies are eligible for subsidy—both capital and revenue—from their state governments through the appropriate departments, and also from the Australian Commonwealth Government under the Handicapped Persons (Assistance) Act 1974, and also (for schools) from the federal government's Schools Commission, and (for long-stay homes) under the Aged or Disabled Persons homes Act 1974.

It is, however, clear that no satisfactory mechanism exists to promote well-coordinated involvement of federal and state government departments with the voluntary bodies. There is evidence of both overlap and gaps in the overall service as a result, and in most states it seems likely that financial inputs are being inefficiently used.

Smaller Non-federal Countries

Statistically-speaking, these are of course the "most typical", simply because the description covers the vast majority of the countries of the world, so long as the term "smaller" refers to population without regard to density. Since later in this volume we shall be giving special attention to the problems and contributions of Third World countries, the present focus can be directed to some examples of differing service-delivery (or need-meeting) structures elsewhere. This could mean "in Europe" but some significant contrast will be achieved by including Israel and New Zealand, to which country we now turn.

New Zealand

The structural model here is one of a developing partnership between the government and the voluntary sector, where the latter is mainly represented by a strong national body with a regional organization. Within the framework of a national health service, in which all hospital care and treatment is free, most of the early needs—from detection onwards—on the medical side are likely to be met more or less satisfactorily, with local variations. But the New Zealand Society for the Intellectually Handicapped (IHC) is "in from the beginning", sharing in the task of parent counselling and providing "family homes" and preschool centres.

Intellectually handicapped children and adults who cannot be cared for at home have until recently been admitted to what the NZ Ministry of Health uniquely calls "psychopaedic" hospitals, operated by local hospital boards within the health service structure. When space in these was inadequate, recourse was had to ordinary psychiatric hospitals where an attempt is made to provide appropriate services. Since 1974, however, the government has entered into a joint effort with the IHC to develop fully a pattern of community services—residential, educational, vocational. To make this possible, the government has accepted responsibility for the full capital cost of facilities, and for two-thirds of the costs of operating them.

The government involvement is channelled through three ministries: health, education and social welfare, and the IHC has direct dealings with each of them. It should be noted that school attendance is only compulsory (and free) for "educable retarded" children through the usual age-range 6–15 years. Such mildly retarded children are usually transferred to special classes within ordinary schools at the age of 7 years. All other ("intellectually handicapped") children are catered for in occupation centres, provided by local education boards where there are 12 or more such children, or by the IHC for smaller groups, the education board being responsible for everything except providing the building itself. Selection for admission to both public and private schools and occupation centres is carried out by psychologists of the Education Department. These assess both social and intellectual development and serve as consultants to the teachers. Later they cooperate with Health Service colleagues and with the voluntary agencies to make assessments and to give advice about school-leaver placement.

Since the educational provision by the state system for those recognized as "intellectually handicapped" falls far short of what is regarded as satisfactory, this question has been under active review. It was "junior training centres" that were phased out in Britain under the Education (Handicapped Children) Act of 1970.

Apart from the on-site workshops of the four "psychopaedic" hospitals, the bulk of the workshop-type training is provided through the "Opportunity Workshops" of the IHC. Very few go on to open or enclave (work-station) employment, and current social welfare benefits legislation is seen by the IHC as an obstacle to employer experimentation.

In 1979 the IHC published a "Philosophy and policy statement" which makes it clear that the Society is wholly committed to the full integration of intellectually handicapped people in the ordinary life of the community, and to legitimately exploiting its already well-developed partnership with government in working towards this goal. In 1970, the IHC provided about 250 residential places in hostels located in the community; by 1980 this figure had risen to nearly 1000, but consequent upon the 1979 policy statement further provision is certain to make greater use of ordinary housing accommodation.

Israel

Since 1969, Israel has entrusted the control and development of its services for all intellectually disabled persons to what is known as the "Service for the Retarded". This is based in the Ministry of Labour and Social Affairs, and is responsible for deciding policy and procedures, and for guiding and advising service units. Under a Director, there are four chief officers—medical care; supervision of residential institutions (functional for government and public, surveillance for private); regionally-based welfare; and psychological services.

The regional supervision of community services operates through the local authority social services, giving instructions to the local bureaux, initiating the establishment of new services, and dealing with residential placement, following decisions reached in the multidisciplinary regional diagnostic centres, of which there are four. Associated with these centres are "diagnostic committees", which have a special responsibility towards persons against whom criminal proceedings are taken where there is any possibility that intellectual impairment is involved. The committee studies the material received, interviews the suspected person, ensures that tests are carried out, and reaches a decision as to whether the person is capable of standing trial. Finally, the national Service controls "community treatment frameworks"; these include the education in special schools and special classes in ordinary schools; day-care centres, for various ages and levels of intellectual disablement; and occupational rehabilitation centres or sheltered workshops for those aged 14 and over who are assessed as being "mildly or moderately retarded". Clubs are situated not far from each of these, in public community centres or sometimes in a separate building. These are run by "social instructors" for those intellectually disabled persons who live with their families or in other ordinary accommodation within the community.

Community-based accommodation includes foster-families for children, and group homes and hostels for adults. Group homes can take from five to ten adults in a foster-family type of living, while hostels are for up to sixteen adults who are able to live almost entirely independently, usually working on the open labour market but only partially self-supporting financially. Hostels are staffed with a house-mother aided by "social instructors". Since about 1978, the Service has initiated local arrangements for groups of 5–8 people to live in houses or flats in ordinary residential areas. Such residents work in regular employment or in semi-sheltered settings, and their social life is intended to be that of the community around where they live.

Short-term and emergency residential care for both children and adults is usually provided in small units (10–20 residential places) which are located in residential institutions. In Israel, the latter range in size from 15–400 residents and number about sixty, of which eighteen are privately operated under service surveillance. Given the small size of the country and the regional organization, the distance from the usual family or other home to the nearest short-term care unit can be reasonably short.

The role of the voluntary sector in Israel, at both national and local level, is complementary to that of the national Service for the

Retarded. Parents' committees are active within each institution, and local branches of the national association coordinate parental and community activity. The voluntary sector does not contribute to service provision, other than in such contexts as summer camps. It provides an active national and local "lobby", particularly with regard to legislation and the citizen rights of intellectually disabled people.

Eire

Any review of the structure of services for the intellectually impaired person in the Republic of Ireland revolves around the dominant role of a multitude of voluntary organizations. There are no less than forty-three such organizations affiliated to the National Association for the Mentally Handicapped in Ireland (NAMHI). These include at least eight Roman Catholic religious orders providing residential services, sometimes with associated day services. These voluntary (or "private") organizations are almost totally financed by the state, primarily through the Departments of Health and of Education, but many also engage in public fund-raising in order to extend and improve their physical facilities. The larger ones employ substantial numbers of medical, psychological, paramedical and other professional staff as well as care assistants and ancillary workers.

There are eight regional Health Boards in Ireland, of which four are known to have appointed "directors of services for the mentally handicapped", and a fifth such appointment has been proposed. In two of these regions, the director was appointed jointly by the Health Board and the major voluntary organization in the area concerned. All Health Boards have a liaison committee to include representatives of the voluntary bodies; these committees are perceived as a form of "coordinating body". The current general policy of the Government is to encourage voluntary organizations to develop services, so long as they are in a position to do so, and so long as they are prepared to develop in accordance with government policy. This policy has been under review for some considerable time, and it is at present only possible to say confidently that in so far as it is reasonable to do so, the "mentally handicapped" should be retained in the community, and that community services should be strengthened to facilitate this. A role is seen for small hostels with an upper limit of ten places, and for "community workshops" to cater for all adults with all types of disablement.

Despite the foregoing, it seems clear at the time of writing that, apart from special education, the main government policy and planning locus is in the Department of Health and its regional Health Boards. There is almost no role as yet for other departments or for local government and its relevant bodies. The heavy dependence on the private voluntary organizations places on them most of the responsibility for innovation, and in particular for the furtherance of genuine community-based services. The Irish structure of service provision seems adverse to a firm and final departure from a "medical model" which continues to regard the intellectually impaired person as "chronically sick", but here it is perhaps salutary to recall the dramatic transformation of the Queensland state services philosophy and practice—from within the Health Commission.

The Netherlands

Services for intellectually impaired persons in this geographically-small but densely-populated European country (14 million) are provided within a model determined by what can fairly be described as a "national philosophy". The role of government in the fields of health, education and social welfare is limited to the promotion of good services by financial and administrative means, leaving the tasks of planning and actually providing the facilities and services to the general public, through the organizations and agencies which it brings into being. Service provision is consequently mainly in the hands of private non-profit-making bodies, rather than in the hands of the national, regional or local public authorities.

These organizations are, for historical reasons, usually based on religious or philosophic principles, which has produced a tripartite system: Roman Catholic, Protestant, non-denominational. Since the distribution of the population in respect of these three allegiances is not random across the country, there are areas in which one of them provides most of the services while accepting clients from one or both of the two other groups. On the other hand, there are also areas where two or even all three are providing parallel but not necessarily comparable patterns of service.

Until relatively recent times, little or no attempt seems to have been made to devise a general administrative policy, with appropriate legislation to cover planning and financial provision, at the level of national government. Each of the four ministries most involved in the problems of intellectually impaired children and adults has gone its separate way, with little or no coordination. This means that a large private organization involved in the provision of residential, educational, social and vocational services in a given area, must deal separately with the ministry through which the funds for each particular service are controlled. Originally, the government funding was entirely through direct subsidy, but in the last decade this has been reduced through the operation of a national system of social insurance, supplemented where necessary by public assistance funds paid direct to the handicapped person (or the parents or other appropriate representative).

For long-stay residential accommodation, the Ministry of Health is the principal source, and it operates entirely through the private non–profit-making organizations. The Ministry of Education's special schools are provided through both local education authorities and private agencies, under a common inspectorate. The Ministry of Culture, Recreation and Social Welfare is the supporting source for all community-based services, including adult day-care centres, through private agencies, and the Ministry of Social Affairs administers and funds the system of sheltered workshops through local authorities only, supervised by regional consultants employed by the Ministry. This system was created by the Social Employment Act of 1970, which covers the mentally ill, the physically disabled and the intellectually disabled from the age of 18 years (or later, for leavers from special schools at 19 or 20).

It will be evident that the structural model in the Netherlands is unusually complex and inherently difficult to change. Since 1970, the very large number of national organizations, generated by the tripartite service-provision "system", have been members of a single national coordinating body, The Dutch National Association for the Care of the Mentally Retarded. Without prejudice to the activities of the member organizations, this coordinating body (known as NOZ, from the title in Dutch) is able to represent the interests of the service providers as a whole, vis-a-vis the various government officials, committees and ministries. The four key ministries all have observers on the Board and Council of NOZ. Similarly, NOZ is represented on the government's Interdepartmental Steering Committee on Policy for the Handicapped. Closely associated with NOZ is the Bishop Bekkers Institute (for the promotion of research on intellectual impairment and consequent handicap).

These potential "agents for change" face in 1982 the possibility of even greater problems, if the already once-postponed decentralization of social welfare funding occurs in 1983. This will involve dealing at a policy and planning level—so far as all community-based services are concerned—with the local authorities instead of with the Ministry. Here it should be noted that the other relevant ministries do *not* have completed plans for a similar decentralization; for example, the Ministry of Health has been studying the possibility for about 15 years.

Denmark and Sweden

Anyone in any way concerned with the needs of intellectually-impaired children and adults will be aware to some extent of the pioneering role of these two Scandinavian (or Nordic) countries. They are included here mainly because until very recently the service structures of the two countries differed in one important respect. In Denmark, from 1959 until the end of 1979, there was a special system at national level for services to the intellectually disabled members of the population, with its own comprehensive special legislation. This provided for a national and regional administrative structure, with regional multidisciplinary teams working within the framework of planning and coordination provided by a central government agency located in the Ministry of Social Affairs. Since 1968 in Sweden, there has been a special Act, responsibility for the implementation thereof being shared by the Ministry of Social Affairs and two National Boards—Health and Welfare, and Education. Broadly speaking, the two boards deal with control, planning and quality setting. But the *executive* responsibility rests in Sweden with the 26 County Councils, with populations ranging from about 60 000 to half a million (apart from Stockholm, with a population well in excess of $1^{1}/_{2}$ million).

In Denmark in 1970 the local and regional political-administrative units were made larger so that they could handle more of their own affairs. This reflected a national political wish to have more decisions taken at local rather than at national level. This reform was followed by a social reform involving the rationalization of social legislation and administration, which led to a new Social Assistance Act effective from the beginning of 1980, in which all "special laws" were revoked and the provisions integrated to cover services for all groups in social need. The main principle of this new Act is to meet the needs of the individual without regard to the factor(s) causing the needs. As a result, all the state services, institutions and personnel were transferred to regional and local governments. A guarantee was included that under the new system the same level of resources would continue within each sector—e.g. intellectual disability—for an initial five-year period.

The integration of special services into the general systems is based on the concept that handicapped people are served best when served by the same political and administrative bodies that provide services for the general population. (It will be noted that logically this brings the Danish services for intellectually disabled people into full consistency with their own philosophy of "normalization", to which reference will be made later in Chapter 5). At national level the opportunity has been taken to create a single National Handicap Committee to advise central government. This has a president (government appointed), five members representing organizations working for the main groups of handicapped people, five members from bodies responsible for service delivery, and seven specialist advisers; regional planning, housing, work environment, health, social welfare, training, employment. At regional level each county has a Committee of Consumers to advise local government. One aspect of the "specialist" approach is being continued—and in the case of intellectual disability it is in fact new—and that is the "special adviser". These work in local areas; they are paid for by, but independent of, the public authorities, and serve handicapped persons and their families directly. Their task is to be a sort of "advocate", to help them deal with the system, to inform them of their rights, and to obtain assistance as needed.

Meanwhile in Sweden, the emphasis has been on decentralization (without legislative change) and integration. In a short book published in English by the Swedish Institute (Grunewald, 1974), which still provides a valuable and lucid description of the Swedish system, there was an interesting echo of the Danish concern even from within a service structure operating at county level (p. 61).

> How far is it possible to combine the more specialised care of the mentally retarded (which can lead to relative isolation) and efforts coordinated with other forms of service to handicapped and non-handicapped persons (which can complicate penetration of the retarded person's specific problems)? This is a delicate balance, which demands sensitive attunement to various trends in development. The retarded individual should be regarded only as one among all others who needs some form of support or service.
>
> It is not enough to normalise the retarded person, we must also normalise our services and the entire organisation of services. In reality, the retarded are part of the total community and they can help us in a process of de-intellectualisation as a counter-balance to the over-intellectualisation we observe today.

Data not yet generally available in English make it clear that in the decade 1970–1980 there has been striking progress in the integrative process at pre-school and school but not training school levels. For example, at pre-school level (under 7 in Sweden) by 1980 only 11.5% of 1320 intellectually impaired children were in segregated groups, as compared with 88% of 993 children in 1970. Similarly in the basic comprehensive school system, the percentage of classes in segregated schools fell from 53 in 1970 to less than 7 in 1980. In vocational education, however, which was on a very small scale indeed in 1970, two-thirds of the now substantial provision is in segregated units. Great emphasis has been placed on the provision of local day centres by districts within the county system, since this was perceived as a necessary step in favour of more group home and independent living. Consistent with a relative fall in figures for adult resident in parental homes or "residential homes" (hostels), the percentage of adults in their own residence or in group homes has risen from less than 7 in 1970 to more than 30 in 1980. Many districts (average population about 100 000) have set up multi-disciplinary teams. These activities at district level clearly represent further efforts to decentralize the system as a whole.

From these up-dating accounts, it becomes obvious that the two most-quoted pioneering countries are still "on the move" in their own individual manner. Denmark's legislative change makes the structure more like that of Sweden than was previously the case, but it may be some time before the decentralization is sufficiently fully worked out to permit a fresh evaluation of the two systems. Meanwhile the responsibility at *local* authority level makes both more similar to the British scene, to which we now turn, but the role in the UK of the National Health Service provides an important and until now inhibitory effect on innovation.

The United Kingdom

Britain provides a probably unique structural model, because the public service system which affects the intellectually disabled person is based on two totally independent sources. One of these is the National Health Service (NHS), set up in 1948, reorganized in 1974 and again—to a lesser extent—in 1982. The other source is the "local authorities": Metropolitan District Councils and County Councils. The NHS receives its funds directly from central government via a ministry known as the Department of Health and Social Security (DHSS). This huge hybrid organization deals directly, as its name implies, with social security benefits on a national basis, but has only a research and advisory role so far as social *services* are concerned. These—along with education below university level and housing—are the direct responsibility of local government (the local authorities mentioned above). Central government contributes financially to the local authorities (LAs) through the Rates Support Grant, which is determined annually. The "rates" are levied directly by the LAs from the occupants of domestic, commercial and industrial properties as a percentage of a determined "rateable value" for each property. Apart from substantial alterations or extensions, this "value" remains constant over long periods of years between periodic general reviews; the percentage levied however, is fixed by each LA annually, and small "supplementary rates" can even be raised during a financial year. Until 1981, LAs believed that they possessed an almost, if not a complete, independence of central government control in determining their rate demands, both annual and supplementary. In that year, however, the Conservative government initiated a process intended to dissuade LAs from making what it regarded as "excessive" rate increases, as part of an economic "squeeze" based on monetarist economic policies.

Priorities within the NHS are subject to guidelines issued by the DHSS; though usually followed, there have been some notorious examples of Regional Health Authorities during the 1974–1981 period ignoring the guidelines altogether, and even of deciding to use for other purposes large capital sums earmarked for a specific purpose. In the latter case, it was—and remains—a matter of surprise and concern that this could be possible without effective action by DHSS in response. What are known as "mental handicap" services have since about 1970 held their place in the top three DHSS priorities, along with services for the mentally ill and the elderly. But it will be obvious that this does not necessarily find expression at regional or local level. The problem becomes visible especially in NHS regions where there are several medical schools with their clusters of associated teaching hospitals; but even in less extreme circumstances, the expensive claims of acute medicine, surgery and other specialties can triumph locally over those of the three less glamorous "Cinderella" groups.

Turning to the LA side, the variable nature of priorities generates an almost infinite range of possibilities for an identifiable group such as those with intellectual disability. In the first place, a change in party political control in local government elections can result in an across-the-board review of financial priorities. Then, within the general pattern of a particular party's priorities, there can be response (on an annual basis) to internal pressure groups. Such pressures may take the simple form "it's time Y had a turn: X has been given a lot of priority for some years now". The third variable at local level can be a mixture of the historical with the demographic. One LA may never have had within its borders any institution of any type or size serving the perceived needs of the intellectually disabled person. In that case, all its citizens in that group will have been in custodial care elsewhere, often in a very large institution. Another LA—perhaps bordering with the first one—may present a totally different picture when the time comes to consider the need for local expenditure, for example, to create a community-based service.

Before going further, it should be noted that there are differences in structure and nomenclature as between England and Wales on the one hand, and Scotland and Northern Ireland (taken separately) on the other hand. (Administrative arrangements in Wales involve what is known as the Welsh Office). But the general structure we have outlined can for our present purposes be regarded as that existing in Great Britain as a whole.

When the NHS was set up in 1948, control of "certified institutions for the mentally deficient" passed from LAs to the Minister of Health and thence to the NHS at regional level, and the former "colonies" became "subnormality hospitals". Even with the passing of the Mental Health Act in 1959, the potential role of the LAs remained very small, and no significant change took place until 1970, when the Education (Handicapped Children) Act and the Local Authority (Social Services) Act came into operation. Of these, the former laid upon LAs the responsibility for providing appropriate forms of education for *all* children during the legal age limits 5–16; the latter created social services departments (SSDs) within LAs and their responsibilities included services to the "mentally handicapped" and their families. In 1974, when the NHS was reorganized, provision was made at area level for Joint Consultative Committees (JCCs), to provide a meeting point for elected members of health and local authorities, with officers from both sides usually in attendance. Although basically an advising body, the JCC can serve as the channel for agreed complementary or joint action between the NHS and the LA. This possibility has, since 1976, been enhanced by the central government provision of special NHS funds, known as "joint financing", which can be made available to LA social services departments "for projects which are in the interests of the NHS as well as the LA, and can be expected to make a better contribution in terms of total care than if directly applied to 'health services'."

In Britain, the voluntary sector plays a relatively small part in the total provision of services, and that mainly in the residential field. Both there, and in other ways, to which reference will be made later, the voluntary bodies perceive themselves as small-scale innovators. This is of course in addition to their activities as pressure groups, seeking to stimulate the provision of more and better services by the public sector.

CHAPTER 4

A Unique Evaluative Study

Having surveyed a fairly wide spectrum of service delivery models, we turn now to the findings of what seems to be the only detailed independent study yet made of the services in a large urban area. This was Sheffield, the fourth largest city in England with a population of about 550 000. A famous steel city, it is roughly in the centre of England, 160 miles north of London and midway between the North Sea coast on the east and the Irish Sea at Liverpool on the west. What follows is in effect the story of the largest single initiative taken at national government level within the United Kingdom structure, described at the end of the previous chapter, to improve the services for the intellectually disabled.

The Sheffield Development Project

In October 1968, the then Ministry of Health approached the Sheffield Regional Hospital Board and the Sheffield County Borough Council "to discuss a development project which we hope to mount in the field of services for the mentally handicapped". This approach was certainly not unrelated to the RHB's earlier request for Ministry approval of a scheme to build accommodation for an additional 300 patients at an existing mental handicap hospital outside the city. But more positively it arose from the same "new thinking" that produced the White Paper *Better Services for the Mentally Handicapped* in 1971.

Before the year was out, the RHB had abandoned the hospital extension scheme and joined with Sheffield CBC in agreeing to a six-month on-the-spot study by a feasibility team from the Ministry. This was carried out during 1969; discussions on its draft report occupied most of 1970; negotiations based on its final version (February 1971) led to formal acceptance by the RHB and the Sheffield CBC; and the first meeting of a joint Coordinating Committee took place in early December 1971. The project effectively started two months later when the Executive Working Group (of senior officers) met for the first time.

This historical summary makes it clear that from the very outset the Ministry was committed to the concept of a major *joint* initiative at *local* level, based on a programme worked out and largely founded at *national* level. What were the essential features of the Sheffield Development Project? They were summarized in the Feasibility Study Report as follows:

Basically the plan is that, apart from a special unit for emotionally disturbed mentally handicapped adolescents and adults which will be at a mental illness hospital just outside the Borough boundary, there should be within Sheffield County Borough:

— a comprehensive assessment and advisory service and a system of referral to it for all mentally handicapped children and their families;

— hospital residential units with associated day care units for children and adults requiring a hospital service;

— hospital service "hostels" outside hospital precincts for those requiring limited medical and nursing supervision;

— local authority residential accommodation (hostels, boarding out, etc.) for those who could be cared for within a normal home if such a home were available to them;

— facilities for education, social and work training or some form of occupation or employment to meet the estimated needs of the mentally handicapped.

It is envisaged that the existing services provided by general practitioners, health visitors and social workers will continue but with the latter reorganized to provide an expanded joint hospital and local authority service giving substantial support to the mentally handicapped and their families. It is recommended that the appointment of a full-time organizer of voluntary services be shared between the hospital and local authorities.

The proposed additional local authority facilities conform generally to existing patterns, but include an adolescent work assessment unit which is new, and also group homes and an advanced industrial type of adult training centre which are experimental. The hospital units and "hostels" follow new ideas. The hospital provision for children is based on a 24-bed unit providing for "family" groups of 8 children. The hospital units for adults are also based on separately identifiable 24-bed units but grouped together to form units of 96 beds. The 24-bed hospital "hostels" for adults will be separately sited although it is suggested two could be on the same or adjacent sites. The number of hospital beds proposed represents about two-thirds that of the current national average provision. It is proposed that the caring staff in the hospital "hostels" for children be chosen for personal attributes and need not necessarily be nurses. But the hospital "hostels" for adults will be staffed by nurses. Experience will show whether this should continue. All the caring staff will have had or be given the opportunity to obtain training in residential care.

Those responsible for the report were clearly and consciously endeavouring to be as innovatory as possible within the constraints of a particular situation as it then existed in the Sheffield area. This they did largely within the prevailing philosophy enshrined in the 1971 White Paper. The explicit purpose of the SDP was to enable

the mentally handicapped person *to live as much a part of the community* as his/her disability will allow, and to confine entry to hospital as an in-patient to those individuals who require specific medical treatment, continuous care by nursing staff, or a degree of supervision and observation which is not practicable elsewhere.

To render more likely the achievement of this purpose, the FSR team explicitly looked to the provision of

an integrated service (as) a primary objective of the project (through) suitable coordinating arrangements . . . both at policy and officer level.

They also placed considerable emphasis on the importance of *staff training* (in both the health and local authority contributions to "the new service") and also made it clear that

there is an important role in the service for the *voluntary organisations*, who should be invited to work closely with the hospital and local authorities, so that a coordinated and purposeful programme of assistance should be planned.

Considerable emphasis was also placed on the provision of *comprehensive assessment and re-assessment services* and of new facilities designed to increase the number of mentally handicapped adults who could *enter open employment.*

Funding

Over the last ten years the Department of Health and Social Security (DHSS), the government ministry responsible, has spent about eight million pounds (at 1976 figures) of special funds on the Sheffield Development Project. Of this, about 3% was used for the independent evaluation studies carried out during the period of 1975–1980, to which we now turn.

The Services That Resulted by 1980

The Feasibility Study Report provided explicitly for evaluation of the project to be carried out by "an independent group, not involved with local services", given the task of "assessing the effects of the changed pattern of care on the burden which is placed on the relatives of the mentally handicapped people concerned". Despite the specific comment in August 1971 by a member of the feasibility study team that this evaluation was "a continuing need, not something to be done after the event", the Director of the Evaluation Research Group was not appointed until October 1975. This delay obviously precluded the use of "before and after" studies in several projects. The use of "time series" designs was effectively ruled out by the fact that implementation of the Sheffield Development Project coincided with the progressive local impact of national legislation, in particular the Education (Handicapped Children) Act 1970; the Local Authority (Social Services) Act of the same year; the National Health Service Reorganization Act 1973; and the Local Government Act 1974.

Nevertheless, despite its methodological frailties, what seems to be the first major evaluative study has been made of most services for the mentally handicapped of all ages, in a large urban area (population 574 000). What follows is based upon the thirteen project reports of the Evaluation Research Group and the Final Report (April 1981) of the Director (listed in Appendix I). In the interests of brevity and clarity, emphasis will be placed on the findings rather than on the various methods employed in each project to obtain them.

A developmental approach

The findings of the evaluation can of course be organized in a variety of ways. Given a primary emphasis on meeting the needs of the individual, the method of choice becomes "developmental"—that is, start at birth and move up to adulthood. The Sheffield studies can then conveniently be divided as follows: (a) From birth to school age: the under-fives; (b) During childhood: from 5 to 16; (c) The transition period: 16 to 19; (d) Adult services, day and residential. As one moves up this age-ladder, the responsibilities of the service agencies change in nature and amount. In (a) the dominant role is held by the health service, in (b) by the education department of the local authority. How far this extends into (c) is determined by the age at which the adolescent finally leaves the school system, but in health service terms the shift from "paediatric" to "adult" comes at 16 years. From the school-leaving point in (c) and up into (d), the main role is held by the social services unless the young adult is in health service residential care. But at each stage, one or more of the other services can and does share the overall responsibility. This makes necessary a theory and practice of inter-service coordination; and therein lies the major problem, as we shall see.

The under-fives

Our information here is drawn from two studies (*ERG Reports* Nos. 8 and 11). Of these, one compared the perceptions of parents in Sheffield with those in Leeds, a nearby larger city which had not received any special additional health or social services funding for mental handicap. The other project was wholly concerned with the early development—under the Sheffield Development Project—of the greatly expanded Ryegate Centre (an annexe of the Children's Hospital) as the focal point of a comprehensive assessment and therapeutic service for mentally and multiply handicapped children.

Let it be said right away that the overall picture is favourable, and that this should not be forgotten as attention is of necessity drawn to weaknesses or imperfections in the service. It is obvious, for example, that Sheffield has well-planned arrangements in its maternity units and through the health visitor service. There is not much likelihood of a potentially-serious developmental disability being missed, and the system of reporting to the Sheffield Mental Handicap Case Register (another input of the Development Project) is well established. But it has taken a long time to convince some paediatricians that referral to the Ryegate Centre for comprehensive assessment may be better (for both child and parents) than "hanging on to the case" and referring to selected paediatric specialist colleagues as seems to be necessary. Only recently has there been welcome evidence of a belated upturn in *early* referral to the Ryegate Centre of infants with Down's Syndrome. Despite this, however, the number of under-fives with this condition "known to the services" in Sheffield was very much closer to expectation than was the case in Leeds.

The clear intention that the new Ryegate Centre would provide an integrated service for *all* mentally handicapped children in the Sheffield area was frustrated by the administrative arrangements. When plans were being made for the reduction of the Sheffield AHA from three districts to two, the opportunity was taken to create an Area Mental Handicap Sector and to locate it administratively in the Northern District. Because the new Ryegate complex—consisting of the comprehensive multi-disciplinary assessment unit, therapeutic services, a day-care centre and a 20-bed residential unit—had been developed from an Annexe of the Children's Hospital, pressure from that source resulted in Ryegate remaining in the new Southern District. In the long term, that could well be the right solution if two complementary conditions were eventually to be met. One is that the Ryegate Centre be designated as the key integrating element in a service for mentally and multiply handicapped children—as originally intended—and therefore having a primary responsibility for them, whatever other specialist paediatric services it rendered. The other is that all services for *children*—including residential—provided administratively by the Mental Handicap Sector should be organized on the explicit basis that the Ryegate Centre is the recognized integrating element.

But in the short term, no agreed clear policy was laid down for the provision of paediatric services in the hospital and hostel accommodation under the administrative control of the Mental Handicap Sector. Consultant medical services for all such children have been entirely in the hands of the two Consultant Psychiatrists in Mental Handicap, and the many and varied resources of the Ryegate Centre was made use of on a discretionary basis, rather than as a regular element in the total provisions available. The exercise of that discretion was found to have been very limited during the period of the evaluation studies (1978–1980).

How satisfactory were the needs of the under-fives and their parents being met? Parents in both Leeds and Sheffield frequently referred to the apparent lack of knowledge about mental handicap among local doctors, midwives and health visitors—though there was general appreciation for the other qualities of these professionals, and few specific complaints. This problem made itself felt most acutely during the first six weeks. Only one-third of the children had been seen by a psychologist during the first five years of life, and the majority of these were in connection with school-entry assessment. Some parents expressly asked for more professional help and advice at home in the earlier years. Only *very few parents had been in receipt of home-help service* (and these all valued it very much), and there was *a massive dissatisfaction with the information brought to parents about aids and allowances.*

On the whole, the families of Sheffield under-fives, as compared with Leeds, received more support from social workers; were more able to use toy libraries, not only to obtain the toys but as a valued meeting place with other mothers; and had more children attending some form of pre-school day placement. More Sheffield than Leeds parents expressed "overall satisfaction" (90 *versus* 68%). The main benefits obtained from attendance at the Ryegate Centre (43 mothers) were listed in the evaluation report as:

— frank and detailed information on the handicap and its implications;

— the opportunity to observe their child's performance and reactions to activities provided by the staff;

— the availability of all the professionals and services at one place;

— the opportunity to take another professional along (*e.g.* health visitor, nursery nurse) to support the parents and to give information to the team.

During childhood

An intensive study was carried out by two members of the evaluation team of ten children who passed through the full two-day initial assessment procedure at the Ryegate Centre. Six children were under-fives, two were 5+ and 6+, and two were over 7. Parents were—with prior consent—interviewed at home 4 weeks and approximately 6 months later. General satisfaction was expressed about the Ryegate service as a whole, including the assessment; home visits by the medical social worker; and the follow-up action on recommendations. Many parents did find the two-day assessment tiring and often confusing, but nevertheless felt it had been worthwhile in terms of better understanding of the problems faced by their child and by themselves. The procedure was compared favourably with previous experience at hospitals. The parents (at the 6 months interview) reported that the great majority of the case-conference recommendations requiring action had been implemented, and they were very appreciative of the home and school visits by the various therapists. Many recognized that their journeys had been minimized by the way staff arranged among themselves for several to see a child coming in for a particular purpose, such as physiotherapy.

To evaluate the day-care unit of the Ryegate Centre, two Evaluation Research Group members spent 20 half-day sessions there during the spring of 1980, carrying out a systematic time-sampling observation study. The staff were seen to work very well together with a wide variety of children, most of whom were severely handicapped and needing individual attention. Every child had an individual programme devised by the day-care staff, usually in conjunction with other Ryegate colleagues. All members of the unit's staff were familiar with the programmes of all the children.

A high staff ratio, both overall and in terms of trained to untrained staff, was clearly essential for this work. Most of the children did not interact with each other, and if left alone tended to "do nothing", to "rock", or to seek attention disruptively. Considerable educational skill was seen to be essential and—over a period—to be effective. The unit had succeeded in placing some children into school who had previously been regarded as incapable of such placement.

The overall conclusion from the "under-fives" and Ryegate evaluation studies is that the new Centre has made a significant and valued impact on the Sheffield services for mentally and multiply handicapped children. This is *not* to say that either the Centre in particular or the services as a whole are beyond legitimate criticism, and some of those made during the evaluation studies have led to a constructive response and various changes in procedure.

There are two points in this review which need special emphasis. The first is that the "success" with which services for these children are provided and delivered, and the needs of the child and of the parent met, cannot be wholly evaluated in a necessarily short-term study. Such evaluation ought to be sustained over a period of years through childhood, if possible by an independent team but if not by a carefully planned programme of monitoring. This leads naturally to the second point: the Sheffield evaluation did not, because it could not, extend into the services rendered by the special schools and the psychological service of the Local Education Authority. It could not, simply because no steps were taken at national level in 1971 by the Department of Health and Social Security to enlist the interest and active cooperation of the Department of Education and Science. This is unfortunately no novelty; the joint report *Under-fives* issued in 1977 by the Association of Metropolitan Authorities and the Association of County Councils concluded that

> the fact that the DES and the DHSS seem so far unable to work in concert in the interests of young children constitutes a serious obstacle to the development of the structure of services. There are hardly any signs of real coordination.

It can, however, be noted that the input to the total services for the 5–16 age group from the School Psychological Service of the Sheffield Education Department was generally recognized to be small. In the UK, this is by no means peculiar to Sheffield since it arises largely from the general neglect of mental handicap in the postgraduate training of educational psychologists. When this is taken in conjunction with a policy of professional resource allocation that is heavily biased in favour of influencing teacher activity and school management in the ordinary schools, the observed outcome is unsurprising. But unfortunately it has been complemented in the Sheffield area by the similar lack of input from the clinical psychologists in the health service. They too have mostly received an unbalanced training, and operate within a policy which gives priority in resource allocation to the mentally ill, at the expense of the mentally handicapped, whether child or adult. Taking the two psychological services together, so far as mental handicap is concerned Sheffield has with little or no exaggeration been described as "a psychological desert".

On the other hand, there can be no doubt that the overall response of the Sheffield Education Department to the Education (Handicapped Children) Act 1970, has been energetic and effective.

The transition period

The Development Project provided for "an adolescent work assessment unit (to be) operated in association with the Youth Employment Service, (where) the work potential of the young special school leavers will be assessed over a period of about six months". This was intended to form the base of a post-school system, the apex of which was to be an industrial training workshop; the adult training centres (augmented by one) would form the central core. The focus of the evaluation studies was initially placed upon the impact made by the innovatory "adolescent work assessment centre", to become known as the Woodside Assessment Unit (WAU), and this also occasioned a replicated study (with a 2 years interval) of all the adult training centres (ATCs). No formal study was made of the industrial training workshops, known as Crown Hill Industries (CHI), simply for lack of time and staff resources. It will, however, become evident that what was learned from the four evaluation studies* was particularly valuable for the light thrown by them on the "system" as a whole, and on questions of policy and management.

---

* *ERG Reports* Nos. 2, 6, 7 and 13. Reports 2 and 7 cover the ATC replicated study; No. 6 deals with WAU operations; and No. 13 with a follow-up, three years later, of four consecutive annual cohorts of mentally handicapped school-leavers.

The Woodside Assessment Unit (WAU)

When the time came for the Sheffield Social Services Department to
plan the design, objectives and staffing of this new unit, key policy
decisions were taken, some of which ignored the recommendations of
the Feasibility Study, while others went beyond them in a positive
way. No specific arrangements were made for close cooperation with
the Youth Employment Service (or the Disablement Resettlement
Officers), nor was a proposal accepted that the WAU should "place
small groups in open industry with their own instructors". There it
must be noted this "enclave"-formation was not undertaken either by
the CHI, at the "top-end" of the system where it would seem most
appropriate.

It was decided that:

— the WAU should have *two* equally important tasks: assessment and
   re-assessment of school-leavers and adult mentally handicapped
   people, with a view to appropriate placement and training; and
   in-service training of the instructor staff, existing and when
   newly-recruited, of the ATCs;

— the Principal of the WAU should be an educational psychologist,
   who would have as Deputy-Principal a person with experience in
   the field of adult training of the mentally handicapped. The latter
   would be responsible for the day-to-day running of the Unit,
   including the domestic side;

— "assessment" and "training" should be combined in a positive way
   over the whole period of placement at the WAU (envisaged as
   likely to range from a few weeks to several months, on an
   individual basis), so that capacity to benefit from one-to-one
   supervised training became an integral part of the assessment
   process.

*It seems reasonably clear that the WAU succeeded in making training the
main vehicle for the assessment of latent potentialities, both social and
intellectual,* in relation to an ultimate target of maximum independence
in adult life. But as to the longer-term "success" of that approach, it is
harder to be definite. That emphatically does not imply doubt; it is
simply a problem of obtaining wholly satisfactory evidence. The
search for that evidence must take into account the findings of the two
ATC studies and of the four-cohort follow-up study of school-leavers.

These in turn lay emphasis on the interaction between the two WAU objectives—assessment, and in-service training of ATC staff—because there is a very large common element, which is of course the "training" method of assessment referred to above.

The reports provide evidence of WAU impact on ATC staff, notably in the use of written individual training plans, greater specificity in their aims, a more optimistic outlook about possibilities in trainees, and an enlarged perception of their own role. But many admitted difficulty in putting their newly-acquired methods and insights into action "back at the ranch". While recognizing that WAU and ATC situations differ both in scale and in organizational complexity, *it seems clear that for in-service training to have its full effect all levels of staff need to be exposed to—and to have largely accepted—whatever is novel about the philosophy and methods with which that training is concerned.*

One consequence of passing through the original assessment period should have been a series of review assessments for each individual, at intervals determined during the previous "case conference". These intervals were usually six or twelve months, and the review could take place at the WAU or at the ATC, as seemed appropriate in each case. *Evidence was found that this system had not been operating dependably, and that the causes lay more in the staffing problems faced by upper management than at the level of the assessment unit and the training centres.* The effects were of course felt most by the young handicapped adults who became "stuck" in the system, instead of being enabled to develop the competences they needed in order to move through it towards independent living.

Overloading of the WAU principal and the absence of supporting professional staff also led to another example of sound planning which could not be fully realized in practice. The principal of the WAU had from the outset intended to involve parents actively in ways other than the purely "social", through the medium of "parents workshops", and to extend this programme into the ATCs. *In the event, there was—four years later—clear evidence of a need for a well-planned programme to convince parents that they are welcome and needed in the whole ATC-based operation, not just as fund-raisers and at purely social events.* The follow-up study (*ERG Reports* No. 13) emphasized "the importance of those at home and those at the day placements working closely together as a team, each partner understanding the problem of the other, both sides reinforcing one another's methods and efforts. The ATC is not a 'school', but neither is it a 'place of employment'."

Services for adults

The planning, commissioning and building to full operation of the Woodside Assessment Unit in Sheffield was such a genuine innovation that it became both possible and essential to have a section of this account entitled "The transition period". We have therefore already begun to describe part of the day services for adults, most of whom in Sheffield are found places in an ATC. It seems logical to continue with the day services, before turning to residential provision for adults.

Day services
Sheffield has five ATCs which between them provide places for about 530 adults; to this total can be added the 40 "transitional" places in the WAU and the 120 places (which are intended—over much longer periods—also to be "transitional") in the industrial training centre (Crown Hill Industries), making a grand total just short of 700. *No unit in this system makes any planned provision for very profoundly handicapped or severely emotionally disturbed or hyperactive adults who are living in their family home.* Provision for these adults was intended by the planners of the Sheffield Development Project to be made in the two new-type 96-bed hospitals, as part of their own day activities programme. The unfortunate combination of staffing difficulties with unsuitable build-ing design resulted by late 1980 in an effective absence of provision for most of these adults needing special day facilities, with obvious consequences for their parents and relatives at home.

Even the one large new ATC provided in late 1975 under the Development Project was so ill-designed that it experiences great difficulty in accommodating trainees with physical handicaps. There is, for example, only one small lift to the upper floor; it can take only one wheelchair, and the controls are above the reach of a seated adult. Not surprisingly, safety regulations permit only two adults in wheel-chairs to be on the upper floor at any one time.

The Evaluation Research Group carried out a replicated study, with a two-year interval, of the attitudes and activities of the staff in the ATCs. The same two ERG members carried out the time-sampling observations and individual interviews on the two occasions (*ERG Reports*, Nos. 2 and 7). Evidence of change, in both the pattern of activities and in some attitudes of staff, over the two-year period was obtained. More staff time, as observed in 1979, was spent in activity which involves a direct relationship with individual trainees than was the case in 1977. This was consistent with staff reponses to an open-ended question about the "aims of ATCs". By 1979 there was evidence of more concentration on actual social skills needed to achieve some measure of independence, and on the importance of work skills, coupled with a very marked reduction in the number of staff who perceived the ATC as a place where mentally handicapped adults should be "kept occupied". This whole process was almost certainly facilitated by an increased emphasis on outdoor pursuits of various kinds, and by the fact that most staff had begun to help on a routine basis in sections other than their own.

In 1979, the forty-four staff interviewed were unanimous that *their centres did not get enough support from outside professional people*. Among the 58 specific suggestions made there was a clear emphasis on "doctors" (used generically), speech therapists and social workers. It seemed reasonable to infer that most of these ATC staff had come to see their centre as part of what *should* be a wider multi-disciplinary service to the mentally handicapped adult; in organizational terms as much more analogous to a school, and quite different from a factory or other employment setting.

Some changes in practice and in attitudes must have resulted from decisions by ATC managers and by middle and upper management in the social services department, taken during the two-year interval between the ERG studies. Decisions at these various management levels were probably affected, consciously or otherwise, both by the findings of the first ERG report and by the working out of the WAU philosophy and methods. Other changes—and the extent to which changes due to management policy were implemented—can reasonably be attributed more directly to the general work of the WAU within the system as a whole, and not solely to the effect on 22 (of the 44) instructors of their participation in the WAU in-service training programme.

Residential services
The evidence under this heading comes from four *ERG Reports*: Nos. 4 and 12 dealing with all NHS and local authority provision, No. 9 with local authority unstaffed group homes, and No. 10 with short-term relief and emergency residential care for both children and adults usually living at home. The Feasibility Study Report (FSR) for the Sheffield Development Project (SDP) recommended the provision of 312 places for adults in hospital and NHS hostel units, and 350 places in local authority hostels and group homes. The 312 NHS places were to be divided between (a) two 96-bed units, to be sited on the north and south sides of the City; (b) four hostels with 24 places each; and (c) a 24-bed unit for emotionally disturbed adolescents and adults.

In practice, the latter was replaced by an additional ordinary hostel under (b). This resulted from a DHSS decision to create regional centres for such residents, which would not cater solely or even mainly for intellectually handicapped people. Of the 350 local authority places proposed, by the end of 1980, 143 had been provided in hostels and 29 in group homes. The FSR proposals made no new provision for the long-stay residents in the old hospitals who had originated from outside the Sheffield area.

As a result, by 1980 this group—numbering about 270, many of them elderly—posed an additional problem over and above the shortfall in local authority places indicated above. Since local authorities are not bound to accept from the NHS persons originating elsewhere, the situation has clear implications for the rate of closure of old hospitals.

The authors of the FSR identified three categories of adult resident, and assigned them to three types of provision, as follows.

— *In the new 96-bed hospitals*, "those who, because of additional heavy physical handicap, or severe behaviour problems, require the support of a full hospital service fairly close at hand".

— *In the new 24-bed NHS hostels*, "those who, because of less obvious physical handicaps, possibly some degree of incontinence and behaviour problems, require limited medical and nursing supervision".

— *In local authority hostels and group homes*, "those who could be cared for within a normal home if such a home were available to them".

The evaluation studies made it clear that residents in different types of provision did *not* conform to the intended pattern. While the new 96-bed hospital units had generally more dependent residents than either NHS or LA hostels, there were similar people still to be found in the old hospitals. More importantly, there were also similar people to those found in both sorts of hostels resident in the old hospital units, and *there was certainly no clear distinction to be found between the NHS and LA hostels themselves*. So far as these were concerned, the major deciding factor for their admissions did not seem to be have been related to the ability levels of individuals or to any degree or type of behaviour disorder, but rather to *the sources from which the individual referrals had come*. The ERG team observed that "it is scarcely surprising that an LA hostel is not viewed as "progress" by NHS hostel staff, when both types of unit have in many respects comparable sets of residents".

Turning to the outcome of a very detailed study of the local authority's five *unstaffed group homes*, which accommodated 29 men and women, it was found that (a) previous residential placement did not influence the success of subsequent group home living; (b) criteria for the selection of residents had been implicit rather than explicit, and were generally unclear; (c) residents received their main outside support from official rather than informal sources; and (d) the social services department had no clear policy for the organization and administration of its group homes.

It is fairly evident that although a useful start had been made to provide the group homes recommended by the FSR, the enterprise had been haphazard and ill-coordinated—a classical example of "topsy-like" growth.

Short-term and emergency care

When it was found that the relevant senior officers of the health, education and social services all believed that the "supply" (except in peak holiday periods) of *short-term relief and emergency* residential care exceeded the "demand", the ERG designed and carried out a special study. On the "supply" side it was established that:

— *NHS mental handicap units* (other than the Ryegate Centre) did not have any positive policy for short-term care (STC);

— availability of places was largely determined by the chance occurrence of empty beds in the long-stay hospitals and hostels;

— despite the fact that all are medical units, the available STC places for multiply-handicapped adults were few;

— *on the local authority side*, five adult hostels could provide between them a minimum of *eight* designated beds, which might be increased by the temporary availability of long-term beds;

— four LA units could, between them, cater for a *maximum* of about 28 children and adolescents in STC;

— *there was no evidence at the time of any effort to achieve inter-service coordination of STC provision.*

With the notable exception of the Ryegate Centre, in *none* of the three services was it perceived as important to *make known to parents* the STC available, or *to develop it as a significant supportive service* to the families of mentally or multiply handicapped people.

Evidence on the "demand" side was obtained through home interviews with one or both parents in a stratified random sample ($N = 103$), drawn from the Sheffield Mental Handicap Case Register. It was found that the main factors *promoting* uptake of available STC were ease of arranging; becoming a "regular" at a particular unit; the quantity and quality of information provided about available STC.

The main factors *militating against* use were:

— lack of appropriate initiating action by the potential STC-providing service or units;

— inability or unwillingness of many adult units to accept non-ambulant or "difficult" cases;

— on the adult side, dependence on "casual vacancies" in a long-stay system, resulting in some "unacceptable places" as perceived by parents, and (especially in NHS units) reduced probability of STC being available later in a familiar unit;

— inadequate and sporadic contact between parents and relevant professional people, notably general practitioners and health visitors;

— as noted above the absence of coordinating mechanisms on the supply side, both between the services and within the health service.

The authors of the *ERG Report* (No. 10) concluded that:

> Our investigation has made it quite clear that the time has come—that it is in fact overdue—for a distinction to be made by the three providing services, acting in concert, between the apparent "demand" for short-term care and the latent "*need*" for it. Need is greater than demand mainly because the parents and relatives of mentally handicapped children and adults *feel* guilty about seeking or using STC in order to give themselves a "break" from the constant strain of caring and coping . . . we have shown that even those who *have* used what STC was brought to their notice, frequently did so only reluctantly and at the last moment before breaking-point.

The social services

In what has gone before, reference has been made where appropriate to the part played by the local authority, and in particular to that of the social services department. When planning a major study (*ERG Reports*, No. 5) of the role and function of the social services, the ERG team concerned noted that the Sheffield social services department, known as Family and Community Services (FCS), "had a number of elements not found in other local authority SSDs", and also its specially-funded innovatory nature in relation to mental handicap under the Sheffield Development Project. These factors made a comparison with another city desirable, and the cooperation was obtained of the health and local authority services in Leeds. This city was large enough (population *c.* 750 000), near enough (40 miles) for practical travel arrangements, and yet sufficiently far away to avoid any direct impact from the SDP. It must be stressed that this was *not* regarded as a "control" area in the classical sense.

Differences in organization between the two social services departments were found mainly at headquarters level, a number of posts being unique in each city. For example, Leeds had a centralized day-care section which included control of ATCs, but tended to devolve responsibility for its residential units to the fieldwork divisions. Sheffield, on the other hand, whilst having some central control over ATCs, did so separately from day-care services to all other clients, but had a central control over all types of residential provision. One of the common characteristics of the health, education and social services in both cities, despite organizational differences, was *the lack of precise definition as to who was actually dealing with mental handicap.* Apart from the relevant proposals in the Feasibility Study Report, no objective policy statements were in existence for the Sheffield FCS contribution to the mental handicap services at the time of the study (1978). As a result, no measurement of performance against objectives could be attempted.

The outstanding finding from this two-city study, which involved interviews with about 400 staff and over 200 parents, was that "*far fewer differences exist between the two cities than had been expected*". No significant differences were found in relation to parents' perceptions of services related to social, educational or vocational training—or, for that matter—in relation to hospital, medical, nursing and other associated services, when considered overall. The major difference in favour of Sheffield concerned the advice, support and practical help given by the social workers to the families of mentally handicapped people living at home. This was largely attributable to the fact that Sheffield had been enabled under the SDP (on a 50% subsidy basis) to provide each of its seven social services divisions with a social worker to specialize in work with the mentally handicapped. It would be easy to miss the wider implication of this positive finding. The immediate reaction is that the addition of one full-time social worker (trained

and/or experienced in mental handicap or not) would of course
"improve the service". Yes—but it is the "other side of the coin" that
is more important; without the presence of those specialists in the
several areas of a large city, the amount of time and knowledgeable
input available to the mentally handicapped and their relatives will be
wholly at the mercy of over-extended field social workers, *guided by a
mixture of personal and administrative priorities*. The numerically small
size of the mental handicap group paradoxically tells against them in
the pecking order.

Finally, it has to be recorded as symptomatic of the "non–effect" of
the SDP that only half the 174 members of the health, education and
social services staff interviewed in Sheffield had reasonably full
knowledge of facilities supposedly covering the entire mentally-
handicapped population of the city, while one in six had no knowledge
at all of the SDP. This was six years after implementation of the project
commenced and at a time when some of its most substantial new
inputs were becoming operational.

The Way Forward

It was the task of the DHSS Evaluation Research Group to enable as
many insights as possible to be gained from the input of substantial
special funds through the Sheffield Development Project on Services
for the Mentally Handicapped. What has been summarized above
identifies both strengths and weaknesses in the services that have
resulted. It now remains to focus attention on the underlying questions
which seem to have a general significance far beyond the special
circumstances prevailing in one city at a particular time.

At this point, it seems more profitable and constructive to use these
insights in a forward–looking analysis. So far as services for intellectually handicapped persons are concerned, the decade of the 1970s
provided a period in which change in philosophy was not only rapid
but accelerating. At the beginning of 1982 it has become *realistic* to put
forward, as a practical basis for policy and action, what even five to
seven years ago was still generally regarded as idealistic.

If the needs of intellectually disabled persons are to be met in such a
variety of appropriate ways as to reduce to an absolute minimum the
extent to which they are handicapped, an effective partnership must be
forged between three independent sources of support and service.
These are the family; the neighbourhood community; and the public
and voluntary service agencies. For that partnership to become and stay

effective there must be an accepted basic philosophy; explicit objectives; a workable delivery structure; adequate resources; and a sustained commitment. We shall examine these in turn, making use as we do so of the response of the Sheffield health and local government authorities to the findings of the evaluation. This was to set up a small working party, consisting of senior officers from the health, educational, social and housing services, a representative of the voluntary sector, and two professional advisers, under an independent chairman and with expert secretarial support. The working party was given explicit terms of reference—with a view to providing a basis for a "strategic plan into the 1990s"—and asked to report within five months, i.e. by the end of 1981. This target was achieved, and the report of the working party*was accepted by the relevant authorities early in 1982. It is hoped that implementation can begin in April 1983.

A basic philosophy

There has been widespread acceptance, and in some places formal adoption, of the philosophy of "normalization" which had its origin in the 1959 Act which reformed the Danish Service for the Mentally Retarded. In this Act, the new objective was stated as being "to create an existence for the mentally retarded as close to normal living conditions as possible". Enunciated as a "principle" by Nirje (1970), it was elaborated and defined by Wolfensberger (1972) as "the utilisation of means which are as culturally normative as possible, in order to establish and/or maintain personal behaviour and characteristics which are as culturally normative as possible". This, in due course, led logically to the principle of "the least restrictive alternative", which recognizes the right of an intellectually disabled individual to live in that environment which is, at the same time, the most supportive and the least restrictive of her/his freedom.

The word "normalization" has—perhaps unsurprisingly—given rise to some semantic confusion. It does *not*, of course, mean a process to remove the intellectual impairment(s) which are disabling the individual. As the man most closely associated with the 1959 Danish Act put it (Bank-Mikkelsen, 1977), "Normalisation means making normal the housing, education, working and leisure conditions of mentally retarded people. It means bringing them the legal and human rights of

---

* Sheffield Joint Consultative Committee (Health/Local Authority). *Report of the working party to consider the strategic planning of services for the mentally handicapped*. Sheffield Health Authority, 1982.

all other citizens". He went on to express the hope that eventually "the philosophy will become strong enough to eliminate distinctions between the normals, the mentally retarded, and other deviants", and stressed that special services "should be provided according to need, and not merely because they are mentally handicapped".

The Sheffield working party did not adopt the terminology of normalization as such, but stated categorically that "the underlying principle behind all the recommendations is the achievement at the earliest opportunity of the stated philosophy, to which the health and local government authorities are requested to confirm their commitment". This the authorities have done: the philosophy was worded as follows.

> Mentally handicapped people of all ages should be regarded as members of the public, usually living at home or in ordinary accommodation in the community, and as entitled to both general and specialised medical, paramedical, educational and social services as are their fellow citizens. These services should be closely integrated and designed to respond flexibly to gradually changing needs.

The working party recognized the importance of the principle of "the least restrictive alternative" and of an individual approach in its recommendation concerning *living arrangements*.

> . . . the creation of a spectrum of residential provision which makes the maximum possible use of ordinary housing in the community, with levels of support staff appropriate to the individual needs of intellectually handicapped adults. These could range from small units with a 1:1 ratio between residents and staff on duty for the most severely disabled, to an occasional visitor for those living independently or in groups as small as two or three. In between these two extremes, there should be a finely graded continuum of support, both residential and non-residential.

This recommendation immediately followed the statement that "there is adequate evidence . . . to consider seriously the possibility that the kind of supervision and control needed by a very small minority of intellectually handicapped persons would be provided, by nurses and/or other appropriate care-persons, outside a 'hospital' as ordinarily understood." From this, it is abundantly clear that the working party was under no illusions about the medical-nursing viewpoint. It is very hard indeed for anyone with a hospital training and experience to credit that long-stay residential provision for severely and profoundly intellectually and multiply-disabled persons can be provided *elsewhere* than in "a hospital as ordinarily understood". In the United Kingdom at least—and probably in many other places as well—that credibility will only be gained by successful demonstration of what is in fact possible as well as desirable. Such a statement of "philosophy" provides the basis for explicit objectives, both long-term and short-term. It must stand or fall on its own intrinsic merits, not on whether it can be realized universally and equally quickly. It starts with the individual and makes explicit the meaning of "community". For example, this term was used consistently for ten years in Sheffield to mean "out of hospital", so that it became necessary to state publicly in 1981 that people who live permanently in hostels are *not* "living in the community". The statement rejects the status of "chronically sick", and emphasizes instead the individual's right to services which are geared to slow-development changes through the life-span.

Explicit objectives

The best known example in the field of intellectual handicap of an objective which is *not* explicit must surely be "to realize his/her maximum potential". *An objective is not explicit enough unless and until it permits the formulation of relatively simple criteria by which to measure progress towards that objective.*

One important lesson from the Sheffield Development Project, and the attempt to evaluate it, is that agreement on objectives and criteria, as defined above, should always form part of the planning for a new service, or for a different way of providing it.

A workable delivery structure

Even the necessity for both a special Coordinating Committee and an Executive Working Group (at senior officer level) to ensure that Development Project funds were spent responsibly, did *not* lead in Sheffield to a well-coordinated delivery structure and operation. This was made clear in the final report of the director of the Evaluation Research Group, and faced squarely by the working party. It recommended "the creation of a unified service at the earliest feasible opportunity (which) should ultimately be administered by the local authority (i.e. the municipal government), with an input of medical, nursing and other support services, as appropriate, by the health authority".

Recognizing that this target of a "unified service" might take up to ten years to achieve within the realities of the United Kingdom political, economic and legislative scene, the working party recom-

mended a two-tier joint structure for the interim period. The upper
tier would be responsible for joint policy, and the lower tier—a "joint
team of officers for mental handicap services"—would have, for the
first time in the United Kingdom, *joint management responsibility* for the
implementation of planning, for the use of funds coming in from both
sides (the health service and the local authority), and for developing
and maintaining the standard of service.

Adequate resources

Under any system of responsibility and of operational management,
services for the intellectually disabled person are inevitably in compet-
ition for usually scarce resources with other—and much larger—
groups of citizens. This is not the place to argue their case in a league
table of priorities. It can, however, be noted that in the United
Kingdom the group with which we are here concerned remains in the
"top three" along with the very elderly and the mentally ill—both
much larger groups—despite changes in governments and in minister-
ial appointments. This high priority at the level of central government
does not, of course, ensure acceptance—or continuance—at local level
where the spending decisions are actually made.

Costs

It is, however, essential to make it clear, beyond any possibility of
misunderstanding, that meeting the needs of the intellectually disabled
person genuinely "in the community" is *not* a cheaper option. From
the limited costing experience available, a community-based service is
likely to be more expensive in the short term, and at best to break even
in the long term. It is more expensive in the short term because (a)
existing institutions, including many relatively new small ones,
cannot be closed and savings effected immediately; and (b) some of the
essential elements of an *acceptable* community-based service will
involve substantial in-service training of present staff, and an increase
in the strength of several relevant professional groups, notably
psychologists, physiotherapists and speech therapists. Here it should
be noted that, costs apart, national shortages may exist in the supply of
suitably trained professionals interested in working with intellectually
disabled people.

Training

When considering positive change in the philosophy and practice of a
service designed to meet identified needs, it is essential to face squarely

the problem of training. But this is not just a matter of acquiring professional and technical skills: for those already engaged in providing the existing type of service, it is a matter of acquiring new attitudes. For this to take place, the new philosophy must be explicit, its objectives and methods of achieving them must be identified and described, and criteria for progress must be as self-evident as possible. Training—whether in-service or otherwise—then becomes a process of convincingly persuasive reorientation. If it is to be successful, the natural anxieties of existing service-providers—especially such professional direct-care providers as nurses, for example—must be recognized, respected and as far as possible allayed. The "students" *must* be genuinely involved in the shaping of the "curriculum". The new philosophy and its practice cannot be imposed didactically as a dogma. An essential part of the reorientation process is concerned with role definition, with an *augmented* more satisfying professional activity. Experienced "mental handicap" nurses, for example, will need to be convinced—not just told—that their training and experience can be better applied "outside the walls", that they have a rewarding role ahead of them working with individuals and families, in an interdisciplinary team-service out in the real community.

Training implies trainers, and if there are not many of them around who are suitable for the task in an innovatory era, the question arises "Who is to train the trainers?" This crucial problem has been faced by Mittler (1979) in the final chapter of his volume. He suggests that, pending a national college coming into existence, "a start might be made by selecting a regional centre of excellence which will provide a resource centre and a training base for staff development". Mittler sees this in the context of "pyramid training", a model in which "a small team is selected to attend a particular course, on the understanding that they will set up similar training courses on returning to their own area". Then at local level "one of the aims of a local training scheme should be to make available a mobile task force of skilled and experienced people who would be able to provide a series of short training courses, not merely at some convenient site but within schools, residential homes . . . and other places where mentally handicapped people live and work".

It cannot too often be emphasized that it is almost useless—and frequently harmful and demoralizing—to send front-line staff to training courses, only for them to face on their return the opposition, or simply lack of support, of middle management. There is a long sad record of this in production industry and in the health, education and social services. The *first* people to require and to receive "reorientation" are those in administrative positions who have effective control of the use made of "duty time" by front-line staff. There is certainly not nearly enough "involvement from the bottom upwards" in the shaping of policy and in its implementation; but in matters of training, where everything depends on a general understanding and acceptance of the innovations involved, the rule must be "from the top downwards". As Mittler says, we "need to think of staff development as a continuous process which is intimately related to their day-to-day work. It is not even a matter of 'in-service training' taking the form of weekly lectures or workshops, important though these are. It is more a question of setting standards of staff performance, of helping staff to become skilled in carrying them out, *and of providing them with the resources to do so*" (our italics). The relative ease or difficulty with which the chief officers of service agencies will be faced in adopting this "top down" approach to reorientation must inevitably be affected by the overall administrative structure. This problem is at its most acute when the providing agency is a large municipal or county social services department responsible for services to a wide variety of client categories, of which those who are intellectually disabled are but one—and a numerically small one at that. Clearly there must be *one very senior officer* charged with responsibility for ensuring that the agreed philosophy is implemented, that objectives are pursued vigorously, that the necessary reorientation and training are provided at every level—and that those trained are *enabled to use what they have learned*.

Staff support

In August 1980, Hugh Firth—a psychologist at that time working in the same unit as the second author of this book—made a return visit to Omaha, Nebraska, the object of which was "to establish the most effective factors in help and support available to residential staff" (Firth, unpublished report, 1981). He chose ENCOR (Eastern Nebraska Community Office of Retardation) for his study because it had "both a clear job structure and a clearly defined package of skills training for its staff". (This is more than can be said for most service-provision agencies in this field of which the present authors have reliable knowledge). A central research question was "what attributes or behaviour of supervisors and others is experienced as helpful or supportive?"

Firth interviewed twenty-one residential staff: nine managers and assistant managers, and twelve direct care staff. They were working with clients of all levels of dependency, both children and adults. The answer to his central question was clear: two-thirds of both the managers and the direct care staff mentioned aspects of *communication*, and in relation to their supervisors they mentioned *communication manner* more frequently than any other reason why a person was helpful or unhelpful. Firth identifies two areas here in which he regards training for supervisors as essential, if "the isolation and consequent burn-out and turnover" of direct care staff is to be reduced.

> One area can be termed *receptive* skills—listening, taking time, asking opinions, being open to advice, expressing interest, and, very importantly, spending time to both see staff at work, and to sit down and talk. The other, *expressive* skills, include noticing and commenting on work done or client progress, giving plenty of feedback to staff in a constructive manner, sharing their experience, giving advice rather than instruction where possible, and remaining relaxed, non-authoritarian, and not expressing moodiness or taking disagreement personally. Such interpersonal skills were shown to be crucial in whether supervisors and others were considered helpful, both by managers and assistant managers but above all by residential assistants. Training for managers in these skills as part of supervisory training could do a great deal to improve staff support and thereby reduce turnover in the organization.

An excellent and comprehensive approach to the causes and effects of "staff burn-out", which Firth defines as "a withdrawal of involvement with clients, and distancing from them, as a result of job stress" (personal communication), is the recent volume by Cherniss (1980).

A Sustained Commitment

Over a period of more than four years, the members of the Evaluation Research Group met and talked with hundreds of parents of intellectually disabled children and adults, and with hundreds of staff in the various parts of the local services. *They found a sustained commitment.* In terms of a changing philosophy, that sustained commitment may need some fresh targets, for parents as well as for service staff. But its very existence in the forms determined by the realities of the existing philosophy—or the lack of one—commanded admiration and respect.

The failure of Sheffield to make the most of the opportunity provided by the SDP cannot be wholly attributed to deficiencies in the management structures and systems of the principal service agencies. One of the most important lessons to be learned is surely that money is by no means the only constraint in the attainment of goals. Wherever the representatives of the people—of all the people, including the intellectually disabled—and the senior public servants in the relevant service agencies, are faced with something like a "quantum jump" in innovation, their wholly understandable reaction is likely to be cautious, conscientious and conservative.

Despite the harsh realities of the worst economic recession for half a century, *everyone* concerned with the future of this neglected minority of our fellow citizens is challenged to be adventurous, cooperative, flexible and decisive. Then the "sustained commitment" goes beyond the immediate carers to those who make policy and those whose responsibility it becomes to bring it to reality.

The new Sheffield strategic plan goes beyond statements about the basic philosophy and the adminstrative structures. It emphasizes that all implementation must be firmly based on a "client-centred" approach to needs that the jointly-managed services must find ways to meet effectively. The absolute necessity for each and every intellectually disabled person to be provided with a personal programme, reviewed when appropriate to monitor progress towards developmental goals, is set out clearly. In this connection, the desirability of naming a "key worker" is stressed; someone whose *responsibility* it is, within an interdisciplinary support system, to ensure that things happen that are meant to happen—and to know where and how to apply the necessary pressure to obtain action. The role of the citizen advocate is recognized, as is the need to explore sensitively ways in which the parents of intellectually disabled *adults* can be helped to perceive them as such, and to cooperate with the services as members of a genuine partnership.

All this will take time—and require that sustained commitment of which we have written—but it is at least clear that the cost and effort of the evaluation was not wasted. Where there was no firm basis for progress, one now exists. In the next chapter, we look at some of the "examples of good practice" in the United Kingdom and elsewhere, which may assist those whose task it will be to bring the new Sheffield plans to reality, and planners and administrators everywhere to approach their tasks imaginatively.

CHAPTER 5

Meeting the Needs

In an earlier chapter, the needs of the intellectually impaired person—and the consequent needs of his or her family—were considered developmentally, from birth to late adult life. When describing the results of a 1970 attempt to provide a service to meet those needs, the developmental approach was retained, but it became necessary to combine it with categories of service. In this chapter the illustrative material is organized on the basis of the essential resource needs of the disabled person through the lifespan, assuming appropriate general and specialized health service inputs throughout. This approach is represented schematically in Figure 2.

The lifespan is shown from left to right across the diagram, with two large circles representing childhood and adult life. These are made to overlap so that the crucial importance of the adolescent transition is emphasized. The "service" needs, shown across the top, are arrowed down to the central point of the appropriate period in the lifespan, with the obvious exception of that for residential provision. This is focused at the central point of an upward gradient from the family home towards independent living. The sources of "service" are shown on either side of the diagram; in early life these are most often met by the family, which should receive appropriate support, while in adulthood they should come mainly from public and voluntary service agencies. During the immediate post-school period, this should be an intensive and closely-coordinated *joint* effort. The lower diagonal line has been drawn in such a position as to recognize that a very small proportion of intellectually impaired children and adolescents will not be accommodated in their own family home, while a much larger proportion of adults will be accommodated in the ordinary community but could not be described as living a wholly "independent life". The upper section of the vertical broken line indicates recognition of the fact that in old age some intellectually disabled adults who have lived independently will no longer be able to do so, as is of course the case with many older persons who were not intellectually impaired in early life.

RESOURCE REQUIREMENTS

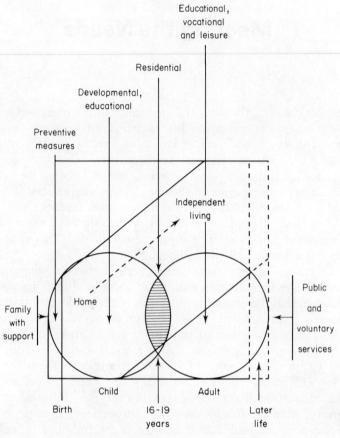

Figure 2. Schematic representation of the relation between potential origins of essential resources through the lifespan of the disabled person.

The examples here provided of ways in which needs can be met are *not* put forward as models to be slavishly copied in all or even most cultural settings. They are intended to illustrate what can and has been done to meet needs in "client-centred", community-based ways. None do so perfectly; the success—and even the continuance—of some is often a costly and exhausting matter for the service providers.

Help for Impaired Young Children and Their Parents

It is nationally accepted clinical practice in Britain for newborn babies to receive an initial medical examination to identify immediate needs such as resuscitation, and any obvious disorder such as spina bifida or Down's Syndrome. This is followed by a detailed clinical examination between the sixth and tenth day of life by a paediatrician with special experience of the newborn. A variety of disorders may be identifiable by then, and impairment to the nervous system may be already apparent on examination. Routine biochemical screening for inborn errors of metabolism such as phenylketonuria (PKU) and hypothyroidism, which if not corrected rapidly cause intellectual impairment, are performed at this time. Where a developmental disorder is obvious at birth, provided the condition does not demand urgent treatment, the first need is for the consultant paediatrician (*not* an inexperienced junior) to inform both parents together, with great sensitivity, of the nature of the disorder. In the case of Down's Syndrome, surveys of parents indicate that the second day of the child's life is the appropriate day to convey the information (Cunningham and Sloper, 1977). The situation demands privacy and time; the early stages of shock and grief, for the father as well as the mother, are not to be catered for identically in every situation. Many questions will be asked, and many of the answers forgotten in the state of shock. Parents will be most helped where the paediatrician remains indefensive towards the parents' pain and anger. Some paediatricians make themselves available on demand to parents in the early days, and invite *them* to decide the intervals between subsequent consultations. One paediatrician considered that the lengthening interval, from a few days to a few weeks, was a good guide to the level of parental morale and confidence. Other paediatricians consider such open access to parents too demanding to be realistic.

The early days of awareness of one's child's impairment are intensely lonely. During the past decade, increasing efforts have been made to enable other affected parents to provide the special support and insight that only they can, to newly affected parents. About ten years ago in Southend (England), a group of parents with intellectually impaired children, together with an imaginative community health doctor, and later the local paediatrician, talked angrily and painfully for several weeks, through feelings of failure, inadequacies and resentment. From this grew a support system whereby the paediatrician, after explaining the baby's impairment to the parents, offered the help of the community doctor with his wide knowledge of available resources, together with that of an experienced parent of an impaired child.

When the offer was accepted, the doctor and older parent visited within forty-eight hours, to supply specialist knowledge but more especially the empathy of the parent who had already been through the experience. A group of parents with Down's Syndrome children, and another group of parents with multiply impaired children, had been formed, and the newly affected parents were welcomed among them at the earliest opportunity. Not all new parents wish to meet up with others initially, or even to accept the confirmation of impairment such association implies. This is recognized, but the offer remains open. This "Southend Scheme" (Pugh & Russell (1977)) with variations has been developed in some other parts of Britain. Not all paediatricians are happy at the involvement of non-professional people at such a sensitive time, but careful selection and preparation of parents for the initial visiting can facilitate a precious resource to those newly affected parents who wish to avail themselves of it.

Concurrent with the local development of that British initiative, was a comparable one among parents of intellectually impaired children in Omaha, Nebraska USA. The Greater Omaha Association for Retarded Citizens (GOARC) formed a programme in 1970 under the title Pilot Parents. It is a service in which

> parents of handicapped children help other parents who have recently learned that their child has mental retardation, cerebral palsy, epilepsy or autism. The Programme's main purpose is to provide supportive experienced parents to pilot new parents through the initial difficulties of accepting that their child is handicapped, learning about that handicap, and finding the proper services to aid their child in his or her development.

The pilot parents themselves are experienced parents of an impaired child, are carefully selected, and given eighteen hours of training. They are usually matched to new families by the similarity of the disability. Referrals of new parents come through several sources including professional ones, and a pilot parent is only assigned when requested by the new family and after careful consideration for suitable matching. The commitment expected of a pilot parent is for one year at a time, during which they are required to meet monthly to share new knowledge and experiences. New parents have their "pilots" for one year, by which time they acquire additional supports and more confidence. They in turn may become pilot parents themselves. The organization, objectives, and methods of the Pilot Parents Programme are published in detail by GOARC (Porter, 1978). Similar schemes of Pilot Parents have been established across the United States, in Canada and Britain. The difficulty of some professionals in accepting parents as full partners still impedes the wide establishment of such programmes in Britain and other countries where consciousness of consumer rights and advocacy is much less developed than in the United States.

A child's impairments may not be apparent at birth, but appear later in the course of its developmental health surveillance.

Many countries operate a system of public health nursing as part of a total public health programme for the promotion of health, the improvement of conditions in the social and physical environment, rehabilitation and the prevention of illness and disability. In the United Kingdom, under the National Health Service Act 1948, local health authorities have a statutory duty to make provision in their area for "the visiting of persons in their homes by . . . health visitors, for the purpose of giving advice as to the care of young children, persons suffering from illness, and expectant or nursing mothers . . .". Health visitors are nurses with a post-registration qualification, the Health Visitors Certificate, who provide a continuing health advisory service to families and individuals in the community, "from cradle to grave". In the UK, there is a statutory requirement for the local community physician to be notified of all new births within thirty-six hours. This information is then relayed to the local health visitor who usually visits by the tenth day after birth and liaises with the midwife who has been in attendance. Health visitors have often already made contact with the parents during the pregnancy. The work of health visitors has five main aspects: (1) the prevention of mental, physical and emotional ill-health, (2) the early detection of ill-health and surveillance of high risk groups, (3) the recognition and identification of need and mobilization of appropriate resources, (4) health teaching, (5) support, advice and guidance during periods of stress, illness, and in the care and management of children. The earlier major emphasis on young children is changing, and the needs of the elderly and other vulnerable groups receive increasing attention. Health visitors are employed by local health authorities but are commonly attached to a general medicine practice. Although the content of their work is broadening, and men have joined the profession, health visitors have a long-established popular and trusted image, being recognized as freely accessible to all parents. The great-grandchildren of the profession's earlier clients are now receiving visits and advice. Because the health visitor is in regular contact with families with young children they are in an especially valuable position to help those families where a child is possibly impaired. The special part the health visitor plays, then, can start from the birth if the child has a visible condition such as Down's Syndrome or spina bifida; or it will arise if the health visitor's subsequent developmental health surveillance of the child reveals possible impairment.

Whether impairment is identified at birth or later, the health visitor will be needed by the family not only for emotional support and general advice on child rearing but also for special advice on the child's condition and future. The generic approach of the health visitor is arguably one of the profession's greatest strengths, and yet the variety and degree of impairments possible, together with the growing range of possible types of intervention require health visitors with specialist knowledge. In Britain, attempts have been made to provide this specialist help within a generic service. At the Hester Adrian Research Centre in Manchester, it has been shown that health visitors seconded there for a training course lasting only three weeks were then able to provide "handicapped" families and their local health visitors with sufficient of the extra advice and practical guidelines necessary to facilitate the young impaired child's development. "Specialist" health visitors with extra training or experience in the management of developmental delay are employed in various British localities to support their "generic" colleagues. Most appear to work with the family health visitors in the preschool years, and some work more directly with families during the school years.

Routine, standardized developmental health surveillance of all infants and young children by health visitors and family doctors in the primary health care team will identify those children exhibiting early developmental delay. The organization of global assessments has been developed and refined in the past decade. In 1976, The Court Report (DHSS, 1976) recommended the establishment of multiprofessional District Handicap Teams based in Child Development Centres as part of district general hospital services. ("Health Districts" in the UK vary in size but on average contain around 250 000 people.) The staff of the Team includes a consultant community paediatrician, a specialist nurse of handicapped children, a specialist social worker, a psychologist and a teacher, with the addition of any other professionals as indicated. The functions of the Team include the investigation and asessment of children together with treatment coordination, the professional guidance and support of parents, teachers and others, and the provision of supportive services to special schools.

They are also expected to plan for development in the district handicap service, to act as a centre for information, and to provide professional staff training. Multiprofessional teamwork in the assessment and treatment of developmental delay already existed in several places before the Court Report was published, and the subsequent style and emphasis of developmental paediatric services varies across Britain. Progress in the establishment of District Handicap Teams has been reported by Plank (1982).

In some districts, children with developmental problems are seen by individual specialists for functional assessments in the clinic and the home; management is then discussed at case conferences. Paediatric Assessment Units were promoted in the early 1970s in some health regions such as Birmingham; these consist commonly of premises on a general hospital site with a day nursery as the focus of assessments and treatment. Nursery teachers are usually the full-time team members, with regular input from physiotherapists, speech and occupational therapists, audiologists, orthoptists, educational psychologists, a health visitor and others, as indicated. The medical staffing includes the paediatrician, but also community doctors serving local schools and baby clinics. The emphasis is on assessment, treatment and appropriate educational placement when the child is two or three. The pattern of attendance varies; for example, two days weekly for six weeks, five days weekly for three weeks, or two days weekly until permanent school placement occurs. The presence of parents at case conferences depends usually on the decision of the paediatrician or community doctors. The final multiprofessional recommendations are discussed by the doctor with the parents. In some of these developmental centres (by whatever name) professionals may establish various local parent support groups. The use of Paediatric Assessment Units by parents reduces when the child starts special schooling although out-patient review continues at intervals.

However, far more comprehensive provision of family support as well as assessment and treatment has been pioneered in certain centres. The Honeylands Family Support Unit in Exeter, England, was developed within the National Health Service as a resource centre for families of severely impaired local children. The multiprofessional team provides a service which includes therapy for developmental problems, a variety of parent groups, home visiting, with advice and support, respite or emergency temporary residential care, and continuing social support from the Unit's staff and other parents. The evolution of the Honeylands service has been guided by the wide variety of needs demonstrated by the families of the children who have all sorts of impairments and problems. Another approach to a single-site combining assessment, therapeutic day care and education, and short-term residential relief is exemplified by the Ryegate Centre in Sheffield, already described in detail.

Child Development Centres exist within the paediatric departments of various teaching hospitals of Britain and provide a regional specialist facility. They are used by families from a wide catchment area, and the coordination of subsequent personal help and support in the child's home district can be difficult.

The delivery of intervention services to impaired children and their parents at Development Centres or Assessment Units may be described as *centripetal*. There are forms of professional help which are delivered *centrifugally*, and this is one variety of support available from Honeylands. The "Portage Project" (Shearer and Shearer, 1972) provides another scheme whereby impaired pre-school children receive an individually tailored curriculum of stimulation and teaching from their parents under regular professional guidance at home. The principle of this American scheme has been adapted and adopted widely. The Portage Guide to Early Education is a highly structured system of home teaching, with sequential tasks prescribed on cards to cover five areas of child development. Home advisers ("visitors", or "teachers") visit the parents weekly and design a curriculum whereby whatever the severity of the child's disabilities, some achievement is made each week. The home advisers may be nursery nurses, health visitors, social workers, teachers, psychologists, or developmental therapists. They receive preliminary instruction on the principles and use of the material, and review their work regularly with a supervisor. The provision of such a home teaching service is not universal in Britain, and is not the prerogative of any particular agency. The Education Authorities of some counties, however, provide a peri-patetic home teaching service to families with impaired children, often starting in the first year. Nursery teachers are often used, and the work is usually coordinated by educational psychologists. The programme of stimulation and teaching is not necessarily the Portage one. Unless the intervention offered is monitored and coordinated by the District Handicap Team however, there is the possibility of confusion or even conflict of advice in the home from separate visiting workers, for example the home teacher, the physiotherapist, the health visitor.

Such overvisiting does sometimes occur; it is of course counterproductive and wasteful and can be avoided by the selection of a "key worker" by the District Handicap Team, on the basis of the needs present and the skills available. The family health visitor should remain in contact and other professional inputs to the home are mutually enhanced with hers if they are made collaboratively.

Recognition of the importance of play in learning, particularly for children with disabilities, has led to the widespread development of toy libraries in many countries over the past 15 years. There has been a Toy Library Association in Britain for a decade, testing toys, providing advice and promoting ideas on the use of play. A local toy library may be set up by any concerned agency, but while often using volunteers, usually it has support from educationalists. In addition to providing toys on loan to disabled children, toy libraries act as advisers and counsellors to parents in many aspects of their child's management. The selection and loan of suitable playthings can initiate informally the unburdening of various difficulties.

The Toy Libraries Association (Richardson and Wisbeach, 1976) publishes booklets suggesting toys and activities for particular needs, for example the improvement of manipulation, or toys for adults who are still developmentally very young. Studies of the play problems in impaired children have demonstrated how essential is the appropriate involvement of the parent in the use of the toy. Almost all parents need guidance in how to play creatively with their impaired child.

The recognition that parents have a primary influence on a child's development and should be central in any programme of intervention has steadily gained ground in the past decade, and ways of improving the parents' skills continue to develop. At the Hester Adrian Research Centre in the University of Manchester (England) a Parental Involvement Project provided parents of impaired children with guidance on how to develop their child's abilities through specially designed teaching games. The help was given in individual sessions and also in parent workshops, where the parents of four or five children met as a group to learn. They needed help in selecting realistic objectives, with suggestions for suitable games and activities and with guidance on the methods whereby to teach their children. A number of very helpful books for parents and others were subsequently published, which described methods and games whereby developmental progress can be assisted in ordinary daily life (Jeffree et al., 1976, 1977a, b). "Parent workshops" have been conducted in many places for various groupings of parents and with varied objectives. One report indicates that the parents of *older* intellectually impaired children seek principally to learn the methods whereby to extinguish difficult behaviour, rather than the methods to give their children new skills, which are sought by parents of *younger* children (Firth, 1982). Parent workshops run for a limited duration over a few weeks or months. Participants usually wish that the professional supervision of their child management could continue at intervals afterwards. The establishment of parent workshops depends on the initiative and resources of local individuals, usually psychologists, but sometimes teachers in special schools. The more regular inclusion of parent workshops in Child Development Centres or their equivalents, could be valuable not only to parents, but also in generalizing the skills of various professionals who would share in the running of the workshops.

In mid-1978 the Intellectual Handicap Services Branch of the Queensland Health Department, as part of its new community-oriented and community-based service policy, opened a "Family Education Unit" in Brisbane, "to provide educational experiences and support to families with an intellectually handicapped member". Its full-time staff consisted of two psychologists, a special education teacher and a social worker. In a paper written two years later, one of the psychologists (Radel, 1980) endeavoured to review their experience, and identified changes made and proposed in the light of it. For example, their behaviour modification course for parents began a year later to change in both content and format, mostly in the direction of "becoming less dogmatic and permitting parents to try out alternatives", and blending experiential learning with formal teaching. This flexibility and the work itself rapidly led to calls upon the team's services from families and parent groups, not only outside their nominal clientele from the Central Assessment Centre, but outside Brisbane itself. The team was also expected to—and did—run training courses for other professionals and non-professionals.

By late 1980, they adopted the strategy of "identifying the needs and characteristics of a particular group, and then developing a specific programme for that group", thus allowing "parents to play a more direct part in planning both the content and format"; they were no longer limited to "selecting from our pre-arranged packages".

Government concern in Britain over the slow progress in provision for the intellectually impaired prompted the establishment in 1975 of the National Development Group for the Mentally Handicapped, to provide central government with advice on policies and their implementation. The Group produced a number of pamphlets describing how to plan and provide appropriate local services (1976 *et seq.*). Attention was given firstly to the needs of children and their families, and the concept of the Community Mental Handicap Team was introduced (1977). The role of this team is to provide specialized help in the home and any other local setting the intellectually impaired person uses. The core membership is a specialist social worker and a community mental handicap nurse. (In Britain there is a separate training and Register for Nurses of the Mentally Subnormal, or "Mentally Defective" in Scotland).

Community Mental Handicap Teams and more especially Community Mental Handicap Nurses have developed widely across Britain (Hall and Russell, 1980). Social Workers have become increasingly burdened by the demands of children at risk of abuse, and of the very old. The intellectually impaired have no rank in priorities in many local authorities, and their practical needs have been identified and met increasingly by Community Nurses employed by health authorities. The core Team membership of such a skilled nurse and a specialist social worker is an excellent resource; however the Team may be very effective with different professionals joining the community nurse, and any professional may be co-opted for different tasks. The Community Team organizes the provision of advice, treatment, training, respite and counselling in whatever settings are involved, and ensures coordination of activities. They are instantly accessible to all families within their catchment areas. Originally, the team was expected to coordinate help to the parents of children at home, but the development of District Handicap Teams as recommended by the Court Report in 1976 led to many improvements in provisions for disabled children focusing on their childhood needs, rather than their severe intellectual problems in isolation. Thus the Community Mental Handicap Teams have developed alongside District Handicap Teams, in some places only coming into the lives of families when childhood is ending, and in others playing an earlier and valuable role in the particular problems of behaviour disorders. Plank's survey of both types of Team indicates that in 1981 maybe 20% of Health Districts had neither Team serving its intellectually impaired citizens.

The admissions of severely impaired children to long-term hospital care have dropped dramatically in Britain in the 1970s. The main reasons are probably the statutory education provision since 1971, the increased provision of short-term residential care by various agencies, and the professional resolution of specific problems, be they incontinence, conduct, or immobility. As many such problems are helped by

District Handicap Teams the remaining outstanding problem in some families is behavioural disorder of a severity not seen in disturbed children of normal intelligence. The attention of paediatricians, psychologists, psychiatrists and paediatric neurologists is turning to the investigation of the part neuropsychiatric abnormalities or hearing and communication difficulties, for example, play in the development and establishment of such very difficult behaviours.

Short term or respite care has become an established facet of services to the intellectually impaired and their families, and when readily and regularly accessible has been of immense help to many families. The facility has been provided in hospitals, paediatric wards, and local hostels run by the education or social services department of local authorities. However, respite has not been available to every family needing it, nor has it been sufficiently sensitive to the emotional needs of the children or parents. In Britain, a fresh approach to providing parental respite has been made in the county of Somerset and the city of Leeds, by seeking and preparing families willing to be short-term foster parents to a local intellectually impaired child. In this way, relief of a few hours or a few weeks has been made available by mutual arrangement between families who become friends. The change in the child's routine is as careful and personal as a visit within the extended family. The consideration of short-term foster care as an item of local provision to the families of impaired children is spreading nationally. There is a small number of children with multiple impairments including blindness, whose physical but especially mental interaction with their environment is very vulnerable in the earlier years, and for whom a change of domestic environment is extremely distressing. For them, the parental relief must be delivered within the family home. In at least one part of London, members of a local Community Mental Handicap Team have been used to sustain care in the home whilst the parent was away in a crisis. One purpose-built 20-bed hostel in Reading was serving 140 severely disabled children (and their families!) by the end of its first year (Klein, 1979), which represented about two-thirds of all such children in its catchment area. The author of this report noted especially the additional indirect benefit gained by the children "through the improved care performance of their parents who had been given welcome relief from the constant burden of care".

One of the main functions of the Honeylands Family Support Unit, to which reference has several times been made, is to provide genuine "on-demand" relief at the end of a telephone line. An independent evaluation of this service was carried out under the general supervision of the first author of the present volume (Evans and Green, 1979; Green and Evans, 1981). Sixty-one families were interviewed which had a disabled child in the age-range 5;0 to 7;11 years during the period of the study (March–August, 1978). Thirty-eight were described as "user" families: "one which had used either the day or the short-term relief provision or both". Twenty-three families "who had been told about Honeylands but had not attended" were classed as "non-users". All the interviews were carried out by Rosemary Evans, using the "guided" technique developed at Nottingham by John and Elizabeth Newson (1976). In 21 families both parents were present; 38 were with mothers only and the remaining 2 with fathers only.

The majority of parents were highly satisfied with relief arrangements at Honeylands. The particular features mentioned were:

— *Peace of mind*, arising mainly from "knowing that the child was happy and being looked after by people who were skilled . . . and who were familiar to both child and parent(s), either from previous stays or play-group attendance";

— Benefits to child and parents of a *regular plan of short-time relief*;

— *Informality and flexibility* (including length of stay);

— *Never being asked for a reason* when requesting relief;

— The "on-demand" character of the service: "*The knowledge that there's always someone there in a crisis*". (There was *no* evidence that families abused the on-demand policy).

It became clear that it is not adequate to offer parents a service once. Families in need "may be slow to become users of a relief and support service. Their introduction to it appears to be critical . . . (and) apparently trivial events during early contacts with the agency can make or mar the developing relationships. *Parental confidence in the service only develops as a result of experience and positive encounters with the staff*, which in turn depends upon good team-work being practised *both within Honeylands and amongst other health care staff*". (Evans and Green, 1979, pp. 194–196.)

While the range and amount of help possible for very disabled children has continued to increase, there are always families for whom the task of rearing an impaired child remains beyond their physical and emotional resources; their children therefore need an alternative home. Permanent foster care of such children has not been given serious consideration as a major resource in Britain until recently,

despite the fact that many foster parents have individually been doing
the job extremely well. However, the Social Services Departments of
some cities, including Leeds and Coventry, have developed long-term
fostering schemes with considerable success, as has Barnardo's, a
national charitable organization committed to the needs of children.
The needs of foster parents for extra training and support relevant to
the child's disabilities are recognized and met in these various schemes.
The natural progression in care of some of these children has led to
their eventual adoption. In those countries where the birthrate has
dropped, impaired children are now included for consideration by
potential adoptive parents. The promotion of long-term fostering
appears to achieve more publicity in the United States and Canada
than in Britain. The Macomb-Oakland Regional Center in Michigan,
the Canadian Association for the Mentally Retarded, and the Trouble-
shooters in Seattle, for example, publicize the need for more potential
foster parents to come forward for screening and training. The foster
or adoptive parents of disabled children will need all the range of
supports locally available to other parents and carers of course.

Another well-established example of the community alternative is
provided by the fascinating story of the Macomb-Oakland Regional
Center (MORC), under the Michigan (USA) Department of Mental
Health. In 1970 MORC was created for the purpose of providing a
650-bed "institution for the mentally retarded" in a two-county
area which had no such facility, and an estimated 1300 intellectually
disabled children and adults scattered in institutions elsewhere in
Michigan. The first director of MORC, David Rosen, and his new
staff realized that it would be several years before the new institution
could be ready for occupation. So they set out to place, as soon as
possible, as many of the 1300 children and adults as they could in
community accommodation. Staff members travelled all over the state to
visit and assess clients, and then went to work on the local scene. The
first stage involved persuading relatives to accept family members
home, on the basis of well-coordinated support services. Next came
group homes and "community training homes": in ten years MORC
placed more than 800 children and adults back into their home
communities. The 650-bed institution was never built: there were in
mid-1981 just over one hundred residents in "duplex" or "bungalow"-
type accommodation at the Center itself. At the same date, MORC
had approximately 300 children and 700 adults in its Community
Placement Program.

The "Community Training Home" is one of the specialized
community-based residential programmes developed by MORC. It

involves the placement of from one to three intellectually disabled children in a carefully selected private home, in which care and training are provided as to a non-disabled family member. "Foster parents" may be single or married, though the former must designate another responsible adult to serve as their substitute when occasion demands. They must have a steady source of income other than that from their MORC services, and must agree to undergo an orientation course (prior to contract), and an 8-weeks, 20 hours course provided through the Eastern Michigan University's "Foster Parent Education Program", one course per year. On completion of four courses, an individual is awarded a university certificate. Tuition fees and travel allowances are paid by the state Department of Social Services. The domestic premises must meet the licensing standards of that Department.

Each Community Training Home (CTH) has a MORC social worker assigned to it, who is responsible for support, guidance and monitoring. Apart from general accessibility and frequent telephone contact, the social worker visits the home at least once monthly, and makes referrals for the CTH to other MORC staff professionals if required. These include psychologist, nurse, physician, speech therapist and specialist teacher.

MORC's specialized foster homes are called "community training" homes because the families are involved in, and responsible for, training and teaching the child placed in their home community. The focus of that training is determined by the individual's needs, and forms part of his or her programme plan, along with the complementary training received in school. At any given time, the foster parents will be working on some of the eight specific areas of the programme. These are: physical development; basic communication; socialization; self-care; domestic skills; advanced communication; community living skills; vocational skills. A method for teaching each skill is thoroughly explained, and guidance and assistance are provided by the assigned social worker and staff consultants. The foster parents are required by their contract with MORC to report monthly in writing on the progress of their client(s), and are invited to the annual programme review to make their contribution of insights and suggestions.

CTH foster parents are encouraged to keep open the communication link with the natural parents (or legal guardians) and the children in placement in many cases will make visits from time to time to the natural home. But CTC families are *not* required or encouraged to develop social relationships with the natural families, as this might interfere with the educational and training programme. If any problems arise with the natural family the MORC social worker will advise, and if necessary intervene.

It is of course argued that there will always be a small number of severely impaired children with such major behavioural disorders that they could not be contained "at home", whether with their own or with foster parents. This is correct, and such children will need as a rule very intensive highly structured management. But Barnardo's have shown in Britain that this can be provided in domestic accommodation, provided staff are carefully recruited and trained for this very demanding work, and given a high level of professional support.

The School Years

No attempt will be made here to treat adequately the whole question of the ways in which the needs of intellectually disabled children are, or are not, being met during the period legally defined as "school age" in most countries. It is a subject in its own right, with its own literature, which neither of the present authors are professionally equipped to tackle. Some attention by way of example has been given to it in the earlier chapter on structural models; this was probably sufficient to indicate the continuing variety of provision, including in some technologically advanced countries a surprising delay in acceptance of responsibility for *all* children, regardless of their degree of impairment, with a consequent and perhaps no longer desirable role for voluntary bodies—mostly supported by a combination of parent effort, public fund-raising, and state grants.

But no one concerned with the question of how needs are or are not being met can today avoid the issue, so far as the school years are concerned: should provision for intellectually disabled children be within the ordinary schools, or should it be separate? And if the former, should it always be in special classes within each ordinary school, or is there a valid case for making these the exception rather than the rule? In the United States, this area of debate is subsumed under the term "mainstreaming", in most other countries under "integration".

Given acceptance of the basic principle, that, to the utmost extent possible, intellectually impaired children and adults should be regarded and treated as ordinary citizens, full members of the real community, integrated educational provision would seem to follow as a natural corollary. But if within such an acceptance of a philosophy of equality of entitlement one looks to see how fully the identified needs may be met, a dilemma can—and does—arise. As we see it, the solution is unlikely to be attained by an approach from the *systems* end which does not entrench the right of each *individual* to a service which most effectively responds to his or her needs. Since everybody knows that this criterion is not met by most ordinary schools in public systems of provision for *non-disabled* children, the chances of it being met for individual disabled children in a wholly "mainstreamed" or "integrated" system are not good. In 1972 the famous "Pennsylvania case" (Lippmann and Goldberg, 1973) resulted in a great leap forward for intellectually-disabled children in the United States, but it did *not require* placement in a regular-education programme. The "consent agreement" actually stated that

> It is the (Pennsylvania) Commonwealth's obligation to place each mentally retarded child in a free, public program of education and training appropriate to the child's capacity . . . among the alternative programs of education and training required by statute to be available, placement in a regular public school class is *preferable* to placement in a special public school class, and placement in a special public school class is *preferable* to placement in any other type of program of education and training. (p. 31, our emphasis).

This recognized the desirability of the "least restrictive environment", but it also recognized that the specific needs of each individual child should be the major determinant in choice of actual placement.

In a review article, Gottlieb (1981) notes that "regular-class education is being advanced as more desirable because it provides EMR (educable mentally retarded) children with more opportunities to be exposed to 'normal' role models", and that this pressure arises both from civil rights workers and from protagonists of the philosophy of "normalization". Gottlieb (pp. 121–122) concludes that

> There is little evidence that EMR children's social adjustment is superior in mainstreamed settings or that children achieve more in mainstreamed classes. They continue to be socially rejected by their peers . . . to be educated in racially segregated classrooms, at least in those school systems having large numbers of minority children; and the daily quality of instruction in regular classrooms does not appear radically different from (that) offered in self-contained classes.

Perhaps not surprisingly, Gottlieb concludes that "normalization as a goal is too broad. It does not lend itself to meaningful programmatic decisions in a school setting".

In Britain the movement towards integration has been influenced by the careful thinking that characterized the report of the Warnock Committee (Department of Education and Science, 1978a). On the basis of its recommendations that the terms "children with learning difficulties" and "children with special educational needs" should replace such categories as "educationally sub-normal", the Committee identified three main forms of integration: locational, social and functional. The first exists where special units or classes are set up in ordinary schools, or where a special school and an ordinary school share the same site. The second comes into being when children attending a special class or unit eat, play and consort with other children, and possibly share organized out-of-classroom activities with them. Functional integration is achieved "where the locational and social association of children with special needs with their fellows leads to joint participation in educational programmes" (p. 101). The Committee (p. 102) goes on to emphasize that

> . . . if integration is to bring all the desired benefits, there must be a sufficient proportion of the activities of a school, physical, social and educational, in which a child with a disability or significant difficulty can participate on equal terms with other children, and by means of which he can come to enjoy the realisation of personal achievement and gain acceptance as a full member of the school community by pupils and staff.

In our view, this is a realistic analysis which provides a sound basis for planning and action. It is a long-term target for the inclusion of as many children as possible in as integrated an educational setting as *individually* will afford them the greatest benefit. In any given educational authority area, its achievement will depend—as preconditions—on the provision of accurate continuing assessment of each child, by interdisciplinary teams where necessary; on close and sustained involvement of parents as partners (the title of one chapter of the Report); and the understanding and commitment of *all* staff, not just those with special training and responsibilities.

The Transition from School

If, as should be the case, a child who is intellectually impaired has from a very early age been provided with an individual programme plan (IPP), and this has been regularly updated, a time will come when special attention needs to be given, well in advance, to the adolescent transition starting at about 14 years of age. The IPP is essentially a written programme of intervention and action, developed by those who are regularly involved with an intellectually impaired child or adult. It defines a continuum of development, and after an initial assessment which tries to determine the nature and extent of developmental deficits, outlines progressive steps and objectives and the support needed for these to be attained. The overall aim is to enable the person to keep moving towards independent functioning. The team responsible for drawing up the series of IPPs for an individual will obviously change over time, but at the adolescent threshold with which we are here concerned, explicit arrangements should be made for a joint review. This would usually involve the parents (or other home-carers as appropriate), the head teacher and appropriate staff from the school attended, the School Psychological Service, the head of the local unit responsible for post-school assessment (such as the Woodside Assessment Unit described and evaluated in the previous chapter), and appropriate staff from any paediatric facility which the adolescent may still be attending.

The decision about school-leaving, and preparations for it, should eventually be taken in the light of this review and the actions and discussions which flow from it, and definite arrangements should be made for the continuation beyond school-leaving of the IPP, including the movement of relevant information from the school authorities to the agency or unit taking on the service responsibilities. In this connection, we strongly support the concept of the "key worker", analogous in post-school and adult life to that of the "named person" recommended by the Warnock Committee (op. cit., p. 76). The concept of the "key worker" involves the identification of an individual known to the disabled person, and already involved in some way with him or her on a professional, social or domestic basis. The "key worker" would be responsible for maintaining contact and for acting as a linking coordinator between the client and all the agencies involved in his or her total care. As noted earlier, the concepts of the individual programme plan and of the "key worker" have been accepted in principle in the new strategic plan for the joint services structure in Sheffield. It was recognized during discussion within the working party that converting principle into practice would not be easy; for example, creating community handicap teams for each of the seven areas of a city with a population well over half-a-million will take time and cost money. "Sharing out" all the intellectually disabled individuals among the potentially suitable "key workers" without imposing unacceptable case-loads is a real problem. But the attempt will be made, and should repay continuing attention.

After School

For the ordinary child without any serious disabling condition, there
are three possibilities when the age is reached at which full-time
attendance at school comes to an end. He or she may proceed to
full-time higher or further education at university or local college, find
employment, or be unemployed. At the present time (mid-1982), the
chances of being unemployed in many of the technologically most-
advanced countries of the world are higher than they have been for half
a century. The difference between 1932 and 1982 lies in the prevailing
assumptions about the future; then everybody assumed that "things
will eventually get better", now many seriously believe that without
acceptance of work-sharing and reduced overtime by unions, and of
reciprocal action by employers, high levels of unemployment will
become a permanent characteristic of life in many industrial countries.

Against this background one is obliged to re-examine the prospects
for those who reach adult age disabled by intellectual or multiple
impairment. Until very recently, hardly any were even considered for
any form of full-time further education, unless their disablement was
very mild indeed. During periods of "normal" full employment, jobs
could be found by or for those who were physically fit and capable of
sustained application to tasks that were not too demanding intellectually. For the rest—that is, the majority—it is only during the last
decade or so that day centres have very slowly ceased to be perceived,
by parents as well as by administrators, as places in which to "keep
them occupied". For obvious economic reasons, the occupation
provided has generally involved low-level repetitive contract work
for local industries, almost always for merely nominal "earnings" by
the individuals involved. The change in name from "occupation
centres" to "adult training centres" or "sheltered workshops" did not
usually make much difference to this state of affairs. There does not
have to be an "intent to exploit", overt or concealed, for exploitation
to take place. Sometimes the absence of incremental payment for
improved quality or quantity of output is the direct result of government rules about social security or disablement benefits. But sometimes the cause should be sought in attitudes which give rise to
incorrect—or, if correct, remediable—assumptions that "they
wouldn't know what to do with the extra money anyway".

This but serves to reinforce the view that the greatest single need of
the intellectually disabled teenager is for his or her educational
experience to be *continued*, and to be tailored as far as possible to
changing individual needs, however slowly these may change. In the

United Kingdom, this has been recognized and fully discussed in two influential documents. These are the report of the Warnock Committee (Dept. of Education and Science, 1978a) and the booklet on *Day services for mentally handicapped adults* (National Development Group for the Mentally Handicapped, 1977d). Both argued for an expanded educational dimension to the activities of adult training centres, the latter document suggesting that the terms "social education centre" and "student" would be a change for the better. While recognizing that "the organisation of Social Education Centres might well vary in different local authorities according to local circumstances and needs", the National Development Group (NDG) stressed that (p. 25)

> The key factor in any organisational structure must be the needs of the individual mentally handicapped person. The most important task is to specify the service offered to the particular student so that there is not, as too often at present, an attempt to meet all needs and provide all activities in a woolly undifferentiated pattern.

The NDG suggested that the role of the adult training centres, renamed Social Education Centres (SEC), should cover admission and assessment; development and activity; and advanced work. Each centre should also have a "special care section" which should not, however, "be regarded as an isolated haven . . . it should be an integral part of the Centre, with the task of meeting the special needs of some of its students" (p. 65). The students in question would be those "who appear for the time being, by reason of their physical and intellectual disabilities or behaviour disturbances, to be unlikely to benefit from the other training activities of the Centre" (p. 68) or "make them difficult to contain in other sections" (p. 66). To be effective, the special care section requires a high staff ratio (not less than one staff to three students), a positive training orientation, support from appropriate outside professionals, and close cooperation with those in the student's place of residence, whether family or others. These proposals have been gradually taken up in different places in England and Wales, including Sheffield, where since the evaluation was completed a "running review" of the centres has been carried out by the Social Services Department.

This is perhaps the point at which to note and discuss an important issue of policy. So long as these day centres are the *only* type of such resource in a particular community, it is clearly essential that each centre can provide "special care" in the way suggested by the NDG. But in other countries—among which can be included Australia, the Netherlands and the USA, for example—the alternative has been adopted of providing *two* kinds of centre: one explicitly "occupational" in the production sense, the other explicitly "therapeutic" in the training sense. The former tends to accept only the less severely disabled, leaving those perceived as less likely to respond to vocational training to the latter. One immediate consequence of this division is that the first kind of centre becomes a "sheltered workshop" in which there is no time, place or expertise for continuing personal and social education. Meanwhile, those accepted by the "activity therapy centres" (to use the Australian term) may get a good deal of almost individual attention in a well-staffed unit, if adequately trained and supported—but there is a very real danger that the vocational potential may be regarded as nil, and that this may persist indefinitely for any particular individual.

Towards employability

The clear advantage of the SEC concept is that a flexible situation can be created within which the responses to behavioural change—progressive, but also temporarily regressive at times—in the student can be appropriate and prompt, without the necessity for a potentially traumatic move to a different and unfamiliar setting. The place for a second type of day provision is *up* the scale, not down it. There are likely to be some intellectually or multiply disabled SEC students who can be helped to respond to the vocational training programmes in the SEC's advanced work section, but for whom an immediate or early transition to open or "enclave" employment is unlikely to prove successful on a long-term basis. For such as these, the *correctly-named* "sheltered workshop" is probably the next positive step in a genuinely developmental approach to individual needs. This has been demonstrated most recently by Bellamy and his associates in the Specialized Training Program at the University of Oregon (Bellamy *et al.*, 1979), following the earlier work of Gold (1973, 1975), all of which was set in motion by the pioneer study by Loos and Tizard (1955). Four assumptions about severe retardation have guided the Oregon work; these are that

— current skill deficits do not imply limited learning ability;

— habilitation goals for severely retarded persons should be socially equitable;

— habilitative behaviour changes should not be expected without direct treatment and training;

— accommodation to individual differences is an integral aspect of service to severely retarded individuals.

(Bellamy *et al.*, 1979, pp. 5–6). Bellamy started with an intensive workshop programme for severely intellectually disabled individuals taken from state institutions. When he and his team had created an operational model, tested in practice, he arranged for replication in differing settings and under varying types of management. By mid–1981, there were at least ten of these new–type sheltered work-shops in operation in the western states of the USA. There is now adequate evidence for the view that very severely intellectually disabled persons can learn to carry out complex industrial tasks, and that they can be enabled to do so *at or above minimum wage levels*. One of these workshops, located on the outskirts of Seattle, Washington, is run on a strictly commercial/industrial basis by three women graduates in special education, with half-time assistance from local housewives. The principal product is sub-assemblies for electronic equipment. Each of the sixteen workers has an individual workbench, and 100% quality control is carried out by a "promoted" production worker who has been trained to use colour-coded test meters. The only task not performed by the disabled workers is soldering; the half-time housewives do this. By the end of its fourth year of operation, this workshop was within sight of a break-even situation financially. For our present purpose, it is important to stress that in this case no necessity arises for trying to "move the workers on" to other employment settings. This *is* their job and their place of work, and they all live locally in ordinary housing with varying degrees of support.

This successful emphasis on vocational habilation is com-plemented in Seattle by a programme of vocational education, under the auspices of the Child Development and Mental Retardation Center of the University of Washington. In his interesting and informative report on this project, Moss (1979) distinguishes between the two approaches, but in so doing describes a conventional/traditional model of vocational habilation rather than the model which is represented by the Bellamy approach. The latter in fact meets the Moss definition of vocational education, stated as ". . . determining . . . what might be accomplished through effective training". The real difference between the two actual programmes lies in the fact that the University of Washington project led to individual placements in open employment, rather than to the achievement of the performance standards of industry within a new-style sheltered workshop.

The results reported by Moss related to four years of training intellectually disabled adults for jobs in the food service industry. Their ages ranged from 18 to 40 years—mostly in the 20s—with median I.Q.s in the 50 to 60 range. Training took place in three sites: the cafeteria in the Child Development Center, the one at the Students' Union, and in the cafeteria or restaurant which employed the trainee after "graduation". The trainer/trainee ratio in both university settings was 1 : 5, and each "graduate" was assigned to a "placement trainer". At the time of the report, thirty-five of the forty-eight trainees who had completed training (with or without any retraining) were employed and a further four were currently undergoing retraining. Eight withdrew during training and seventeen had not yet completed it. The average initial training time was 8.3 months and average re-training took 1.5 months. It was reported that there was "a high rate of employment stability once a worker remains at a job for at least two months" (p. 28). In view of the observations and data reported in the previous chapter, it is noteworthy that Moss felt obliged (p. 36) to emphasise that

> The ability to take advantage of public transportation is essential to acquiring and holding a job for moderately and severely retarded adults. Every trainee in the project reported herein, even those with the lowest functioning levels, was taught to ride buses to and from the training site, and to and from work without supervision.

There is much else in this report which deserves close study by anyone concerned about or with the transition from school to employment.

Towards the end of their highly technical text, Bellamy et al. (1979) enter an important cautionary note (p. 218):

> The availability of techniques for vocational development should not preclude efforts of parallel technologies in other service areas, nor should it automatically result in a primary emphasis in vocational objectives for all severely retarded individuals.

They also indicate their sensitivity to the problem faced by ATC staff in Sheffield on returning to their centres after in-service training; conflict between the habilitation and production goals of the centre. Bellamy and his associates suggest that their model of "direct-service technology" may offer assistance here, "since it raises the possibility that severely retarded adults can become the stable employees whose productivity is central to the workshop's commercial success. A more extensive community placement effort . . . could then be designed for mildly handicapped participants . . . a production focus for the more severely disabled could allow them to earn significant wages in extended employment, while an educational emphasis with mildly handicapped persons might increase placement possibilities." (p. 221) They cite as an example of "A more extensive community placement effort" the project described by Moss.

Against the background of widespread reports—as in Sheffield—of training centres and traditional sheltered workshops "silting up" because so few of their clients move on, these carefully planned and executed initiatives, and the ideas to which they give rise, provide some rays of realistic hope. The same can be said of the Pathway Scheme, which was launched in 1975 by the South Wales Region of the UK's Royal National Society for Mentally Handicapped Children and Adults (MENCAP). The basic idea was deceptively simple: offer to pay a prospective sympathetic employer twelve weeks' reimbursement of wages, whatever the rate of pay; and ask him to nominate a willing experienced employee as a "foster worker" who for the same period would receive a weekly gratuity. The latter would provide adequate instruction and supervision, and become a supportive friend to the person placed as a new employee.

By the end of 1980, 135 intellectually disabled persons were successfully placed into employment in a wide variety of jobs, despite accelerating rates of general unemployment in South Wales. Many satisfied employers refused to accept the twelve weeks' reimbursement of wages, and similarly many "foster workers" either refused their gratuity or shared it with helpful workmates. Employers report that their Pathway employees display highly-valued qualities, such as punctuality, low absenteeism, reliability, and willingness to work and to learn. As a result of the success of the scheme in South Wales, it now operates also in the London Region and in five other MENCAP Regions in England.

How does the Pathway Scheme work, and what is the secret of its obvious success? The answers to these questions are taken directly from the leaflet issued by the Society (MENCAP, 1981):

> The Pathway Scheme revolves around MENCAP's Pathway Employment Officer, who is based at the Society's Regional Office. Mentally handicapped people who might benefit from Pathway are referred to the Employment Officer by MENCAP Local Societies, Local Authority adult training centres, special schools, hospitals and often by Disablement Resettlement Officers and Careers Officers. The Employment Officer meets the applicant and his or her family at home. On completion of an application and assessment form, the training achievement reached by the applicant is carefully considered and a decision made on whether

or not the applicant will benefit immediately or after a further period of training.

An individual social education and training programme can be designed for every Pathway trainee, based on the Employment Officer's assessment of his abilities and potential. The aim of this programme is to teach the trainee about every aspect of going out to work—everything from clocking on to how to tell the boss something is troubling you—and the programme is always tailored to meet the needs of the individual. Because his special programme makes the most of what he can do well, and helps him with things he's not so sure of, the trainee becomes much more self-reliant and independent, and has the confidence to tackle what may be his first job. If the trainee is at an adult training centre, this pre-work preparation is usually designed to take place in the setting of the ATC. Alternatively the trainee could find himself taking part in a work preparation course at a college of further education or a training course at one of MENCAP's advanced social training establishments.

Once the trainee has successfully completed his or her pre-work preparation course, the Employment Officer co-operates with the local Disablement Resettlement Officer and Careers specialists to find the trainee a suitable job with a sympathetic employer. Wherever possible the Employment Officer tries to find the trainee the kind of work he himself is interested in, and this may be anything from kitchen assistant, fruit packer and factory worker to sewing machinist or even hotel porter. Each employer chooses a foster worker to take the new employee under his or her wing. The foster worker is the key person to the success of a Pathway placement, as he or she not only trains the mentally handicapped employee in their new job, but helps them cope with all the other things involved in "going out to work"—finding your way around, clocking on, collecting and checking your wages, eating in the canteen, and joining a union. Quite often the Pathway trainee and the foster worker become firm friends and enjoy each other's company at work socials and outings.

If the Pathway trainee completes his or her probation period successfully it is likely that they will be welcomed as a full-time member of staff with a contract of employment and the same rights and privileges as everyone else in the firm. They earn the normal rate for the job, and have the satisfaction of knowing that they are making a contribution to the community where they live and to the nation as a whole. Often those who benefit from Pathway have failed to find work in the past or have not been able to hold down a job, and are so delighted with this opportunity to make a successful path in life that they make every effort to please their employer with their time-keeping, reliability and efficiency. Of course one or two Pathway trainees don't succeed in the first job the Employment Officer finds for them, but it is often possible to find them another job where they can settle in happily.

The secret to Pathway's immediate success lies in its flexibility and the fact that the scheme is tailored to meet the needs of mentally handicapped people as individuals. The Employment Officer continues to support the Pathway workers long after they have settled into their jobs, and keeps in touch with them and their families. Whenever problems arise the Employment Officer is there to help and is happy to advise employers, making regular visits to see that all is going well.

The Employment Officer works closely with all the authorities involved, and the needs of the mentally handicapped person are put first, all along the way. For instance when an applicant is accepted for Pathway the Employment Officer makes sure the authority responsible for him, be it social service department or hospital, will take back the applicant if he is unable to complete his pre-work training course successfully.

The "enclave" approach

This concept, known alternatively as the "work station", has a number of positive features that merit attention. Basically it involves a group of intellectually disabled adults, working under their own trained supervisor, within an "open employment" situation. The supervisor is in fact doubly trained; to work with intellectually disabled people, and to supervise effectively the task or tasks involved. The most satisfactory arrangement is for the agency concerned to be the contractor, vis-a-vis the industrial or other enterprise, and therefore also the employer of the intellectually disabled persons. In this arrangement, no problems arise for the enterprise over possible legal difficulties such as redundancy payment rights. Experience in the successful application of this approach has been gained over many years by ENCOR in Omaha, Nebraska. For example, one of its "work stations" has responsibility for a major section of the dishwashing operation in the very modern kitchen of a large hospital. No visitor could fail to be impressed by the quiet cheerful efficiency of this group of sixteen disabled men and women, working alongside the regular staff. Another work station contract is for the housekeeping on a whole floor of a large motel in a well-known national chain.

It has also been found that in certain circumstances it can become possible to gradually withdraw the agency supervisor. An example of this will be cited (p. 120) in the Pengwern Hall story; others are available from Israel (Chigier, 1975) and from Sheffield, which has in fact not used the ordinary enclave or work station approach. For several years, a few individuals at a time have been "placed" by one of the adult training centres in a local plastics firm. Each trainee receives initial support from his ATC staff instructor, but if he succeeds in settling down to the work in the factory, he comes under the supervision of the firm's foreman in his section. More recently, advantage has also been taken of a scheme originally devised for physically disabled persons. This enables a Local Authority to obtain financial assistance from central government funds, under the Disabled Persons (Employment) Act, to set up Sheltered Employment Groups by arrangement with interested firms. The scheme provides for two levels of "minimum work performance" (30 and 50%); the contract between the social services department of the Local Authority and the firm provides for the latter to pay the 30 (or 50) %, central funds to meet three-quarters of the balance, and the Local Authority the remainder. The latter also pays for the usual employers' contribution to national insurance, and for holiday pay. Those placed are under the daily supervision of the firm's foremen in their work sections, supported to the extent necessary by the staff of the training centre making the placement.

In all these schemes, the explicit objective is that individuals will progress to ordinary open employment on an independent basis—either with the collaborating employer or elsewhere. If this is to be at all likely, especially in the increasingly competitive "job-market", the placing agency must sustain an active role in providing each individual with appropriate social and educational support outside the work situation. This necessity highlights the logic of the "individual programme plan" and "key worker" concepts.

Open-air options
Just because an intellectually disabled adult happened to be born in an urban area, there is no logical basis for the usual assumption that he or she should be trained for industrial work. Yet that assumption underlies the planning and operation of most urban day provision. Recently, as in Sheffield where this provided most of the jobs for the very few who were placed successfully, the municipal parks department has given a lead. This should be encouraged and firm but tactful pressure brought to bear on the municipal authorities which, not only in Britain as we have seen, have day-activity service responsibility for intellectually disabled persons.

Possibly because their direct service contribution is often residential, the voluntary agencies have gained considerable experience in developing the interest and capacities of their residents in outdoor activity. Sometimes this is confined to gardening work in the grounds of the residence, but some voluntary agencies take it further than that. Notable among these are the Home Farm Trust and the Camphill

Trust, which is based on the Rudolf Steiner community at Aldenham in Hertfordshire, England. The latter has for many years been extending its work for the intellectually disabled in a variety of residential settings. One of these, started in 1973, is Coleg Elidyr (named after a sixth-century Welsh saint) in the mountains of mid-Wales, which includes 200 acres of farmland. An old house, with outbuildings, has been supplemented in stages by additional buildings, to provide for a mixed community of 60 intellectually disabled, epileptic and spastic adolescents, and the resident permanent and short-term staff members. The students are sent and paid for by Local Authorities all over Britain, and stay for three years. They spend the mornings on the work which makes the college community virtually self-sufficient: gardening, farming, forestry, cooking, laundry, house-work. Afternoons are devoted to individually appropriate further education and to craft work—including weaving, with wool from the sheep on the farm which students are taught how to wash, spin and dye. In the nearby village, the college set up a small sheltered hostel in an ordinary house for some of the students who have completed their three years. Living with the helpers, they produce woven materials, run a small printing shop and a coffee bar.

The national society in the United Kingdom, already referred to as MENCAP, has a Rural Training Unit with a full-time director that runs several projects in different parts of England and Wales. Without the explicit anthroposophical philosophy of the Rudolf Steiner move-ment, these also accept students from Local Authorities (but for periods varying from three months to three years). One of these MENCAP centres, Pengwern, is located near the North Wales coast, about three miles from a small cathedral and market town, St. Asaph. It has places for 90 students, 30 of whom—mostly new arrivals—live in the original house (Pengwern Hall). Four living units, converted from old coach-houses by Pengwern's own instructors and students, each accommodate 3 teenage boys and 3 girls and 2 houseparents. Two adjacent terraced Victorian houses in St. Asaph have been completely remodelled and refitted—again by staff and students. In one of these there are resident staff, but the other is unstaffed to provide further experience in more independent living. A further three houses are situated in villages some miles away.

The Pengwern principal (Weinberg, 1981) makes explicit

Pengwern's philosophy is that all training must be designed with the clear aim in view that, when the need arises, these young people will be able to live with the minimum possible support in normal houses as members of the community. To prepare for this, they must have the opportunity of learning to look after themselves in every way, take decisions, and be able to face up to the give-and-take that is part of everyday life. Work preparation and further education have a part to play in this, but neither is seen as an end in itself.

The Pengwern Hall Estate of 22 acres has been developed through its large market garden and greenhouses. From that it is a natural step to employment in the St. Asaph's municipal Parks and Gardens Department. This started as an "enclave" or "work-station" project, but the changing group of Pengwern residents has for the last four years worked under the supervision of the parks superintendent, without a Pengwern staff member. This is a predominantly male occupation, so Pengwern set about to provide a real-life work setting for girls. This was achieved through the acquisition of shop premises four years ago, on a corner across the road from the cathedral, for the sale of groceries and vegetables (including some of Pengwern's produce). The principal tells the story as follows (Weinberg, 1981):

> Turner's Stores, the corner shop, resumed its traditional function with Pengwern's staff and trainees behind the counters in May 1978. The educative opportunities it provided for the mentally handicapped and the public was evident from the outset. Formal attempts to teach trainees to use the till and the weighing machine prior to the day of opening were completely unsuccessful. Anxiety about the outcome delayed the fateful moment and even when the doors were finally opened the worst fears seemed completely justified. Attempts to restrict the girls to supportive roles failed as they insisted on serving. The new till with its carefully adjusted buttons and knobs was put out of action by an enthusiastic but awkward trainee in the first minutes. Shoppers of all ages rose to the situation and saw it as their function to help the trainees with the calculations and change. By a combination of the reality of the setting, the involvement of the public and the repetition of the processes (as well as the patience of the staff) the trainees learnt rapidly. The newly restored till has never been out of action since and the annual turnover has risen to £40,000.
>
> The part played by Turner's Stores not least as a public relations exercise cannot be over-estimated. A major achievement has been in its presentation of the mentally handicapped in an entirely unusual guise and a reversal of their role from dependent to provider. Seen in a new light by the public they were soon in demand for all kinds of other jobs: assistants at the local play-group, home-helps, baby-minders, riding-school, helping old people with their gardens and delivering to their doors. They have a real and unmistakable place within the community and are valued for themselves.

The problem faced by Camphill, MENCAP and other voluntary agencies displaying similar successful enterprise in the rural or peri-urban setting, is that if they are not to become providers of mini-institutions, their trainees *must* go back eventually to their home towns. It then becomes the responsibility of the Local Authority social services department, in collaboration with Disablement Resettlement Officers of the Department of Employment, to seek suitable permanent jobs for the "graduates". No longer is there any excuse for thinking exclusively in terms of urban industrial employment; but it will place a heavy demand on the officers concerned—and on their superiors—for an imaginative approach to each individual's needs and capabilities.

A notable example of a rural enterprise in which permanent employment is envisaged for some of the intellectually disabled young people trained, is provided by the Spring Valley Brahman Stud Farm in Queensland, Australia. The directors of the large state voluntary society, which was already responsible for many schools, residential units and sheltered workshops, saw the need for a centre which would meet the needs of young people born and brought up in rural areas. The opportunity was grasped—not without some expressions of anxiety by society members—to purchase an established cattle stud, about seven miles outside a medium-sized country town. The property included undeveloped land suitable for the cultivation of avocados for the commercial market. The key to immediate success was most probably the readiness of the experienced stud-master to stay on and "have a go". Within four years it had been established that moderately disabled young men could be trained, not only to work with these large animals, but even to handle them in the show-ring.

The avocado development has opened up the possibility of young women being accepted for training, and also for progress in residential arrangements from a single multi-purpose residence to a cluster of small living units round the warden's house, which serves as a more home-like social focus. By late 1981, it had become realistic to start planning for young people in the nearby small town to come out on a daily basis, continuing to live in their family home or in a small group home. At this point, it was also expected that those with greater intellectual disability could begin to find places in the scheme.

The overall lesson from these few examples is that the limits upon what intellectually disabled young people can learn to do vocationally are often located as much in the minds of their parents and of the service-providers as in the impairment which has slowed their own development. "Without vision, the people perish" could here well be adapted to "without vision the intellectually impaired are unnecessarily handicapped".

Continuing education

Reference having already been made to the need for programmes within adult training centres to become more oriented towards social education, what should be the role of those units of the public education system that are responsible for what is frequently called "further education"? In many countries, largely regardless of differences in structure, financing and locus of responsibility, such units are concerned with the provision of all forms of continuing education, after the end of formal school attendance, which are not the primary responsibility of such institutions of higher education as universities and polytechnics. Until fairly recently, many local colleges or institutes for technical, commercial or further education catered primarily for evening and/or day-release students in some form of employment or apprenticeship. Some also provided evening classes in "liberal studies" for mature adults, usually non-credit but sometimes towards external degree qualifications awarded by a university, or a national body such as the Council for National Academic Awards (CNAA) in Britain. However educationally or intellectually undeveloped or inadequate their less able students might be, these units did not regard it as part of their educational role to design and provide "continuing education" for those identified already as (in Britain) the "educationally sub-normal". But during the last five years evidence has been growing that many colleges of further education have been alerted to this new role, and some are making appropriae responses. We shall draw our examples from the Sheffield area, partly because recent information is readily available, but also because these new cooperative activities reflect changes for the better since the Sheffield evaluation studies were completed.

The lead in the North of England was provided by the North Nottinghamshire College of Further Education, which is situated in Worksop, just across the county border from Sheffield. Following a small pilot course in 1969, this college has successfully established a three-level curricular structure for school-leavers, of which the intellectually least demanding (the Work Orientation Unit) caters for 20 to 25% of all students in the college. As the title implies, every WOU student was regarded at the outset as employable, and to render this more likely of fulfilment, a genuinely individual approach is adopted. This uses a model in which a diagnostic process establishes the specific strengths and weaknesses of each student on admission; sets out to remedy the employment-related weaknesses by training; and aims to achieve a level of general social and work behaviour acceptable in open employment. Recently the Unit has responded to changing needs by also accepting students for whom a realistic target may prove, despite every effort, to be "a significant life without work".

All forms of disablement—sensory, physical, emotional, and intellectual are to be found in those occupying the 175 full-time places available in the Unit; the degree of disablement ranges from "minimal" to "severe". Broadly speaking, the disablement of those described as "severe" is likely to be sensory, physical or emotional rather than intellectual, but on the other hand it would be inaccurate to imply that all or most of those with intellectual disablement could be described as "minimal". Candidates for admission are referred by careers officers in the region with whom contact is maintained throughout the student's time in the college. At any given time, there are in the Unit about 12–14 students who, after a three weeks trial, proved able to adjust to the College environment, perhaps with help from fellow students, but not needing constant staff supervision. The college has from an early stage in the development of this individualized approach accepted referrals from the Woodside Assessment Unit in Sheffield, which works closely with the careers service.

In the report of a survey on the "transition period" carried out in nine British local authorities as part of an international project, Rowan (1980) recognizes the reality of the difficulties faced by colleges of further education attempting to run courses for more severely intellectually disabled young people (p. 45).

> The atmosphere at the Potternewton Annexe is happy, lively with resources that emphasise colour and shape and number, and the students are learning skills that will develop their personal potential. But it is essentially a continuation of the special school, and the question of what students should be prepared for is perhaps becoming pressing, since at present few of them do leave the course. With 10 to 12 joining it each year, it cannot remain open-ended indefinitely.

The four other colleges in or near Sheffield now have working arrangements with the adult training centres in the city, in some cases on a two-way system. This involves, for example, staff taking students from college engineering and workshop courses to an ATC, where design projects are identified, the outcome of which will provide the ATC with new special purpose jigs and tools which their own students can use. Some of these in due course go part-time to the college for more advanced training. Students from all the ATCs now go part-time to these colleges for domestic science, "keep-fit" classes and games. Similar arrangements are known to be in operation elsewhere, for example in several colleges within the area of Cheshire.

Adult education

Towards the end of the report by Rowan (1980), there is a two-page chapter entitled "Adult Education Service". Noting that what mainly distinguishes this from "further education" is its part-time, non-vocational, non-credit character, she says (p. 100):

> There are two ways of providing adult education for handicapped people. One thing that the adult education service can do . . . is to back up and reinforce the work that is already going on in FE colleges, adult training and day centres, and hospitals, with literacy and numeracy classes, as well as some recreational activities. Literacy teaching can also be extended to the home where necessary. *The other is to try and integrate them, wherever possible, into normal evening classes.* (Our italics).

In the London area a new scheme was launched towards the end of 1981 by the Metropolitan Region of MENCAP, the national society. A single full-time coordinator works in cooperation with adult education institutes on what is described as an "integration" project. The object is to find out how this objective can be made a reality, and how to make ordinary adult education facilities accessible to intellectually disabled persons. An essential part of the approach involves recruitment of volunteers from the community, whose role—on an individual basis—is to befriend the disabled student, enabling him or her to participate successfully in mainstream classes. It was appreciated from the outset that the volunteer—who is not a substitute or ancillary teacher—would need support and training to fulfil the role. Before the end of the first academic session, the project succeeded in recruiting over one hundred volunteers and placing them and their intellectually disabled student in a variety of ordinary classes in two areas, one in an inner London suburb, the other on the outskirts. The classes attended included pottery, arts and crafts, dressmaking, music appreciation, swimming and keep-fit. Already instances have occurred of the disabled person proving more adept than the "volunteer friend", and it has been obvious that the students' learning quickly extends beyond the subject skills, in terms of communication, social and self-confidence development.

In the "advice to volunteers", it is not only explained that tasks will need to be broken down into small steps to facilitate successful progress, but also that the volunteer must aim to help the student to make her/his own choices. From this it is but a step to the realization that "the work as a volunteer also consists of being an advocate when necessary". It is instructive to note the actual suggestions made to the volunteer by the project coordinator (Billis, 1981).

1. Be aware that the way you talk to your friend will often set the tone that others in the Adult Education Institute might follow. Treat him or her as an adult and therefore try to avoid talking down to your friend when showing him or her how to do something.

2. Everyone needs encouragement, therefore concentrate on the things your friend can do well. The more one fails the less motivated one is to succeed. Therefore, help your friend complete the tasks successfully *BUT* not by doing it for him/her.

3. You should not be prepared to tolerate behaviour that you would not accept from anyone else in the class. Usually your friend will behave as others if you make it clear that you expect this.

4. On introducing your friend to others, there is usually no need to explain that he/she is handicapped.

5. Be careful not to talk about your friend in his/her presence.

6. Try to find ways of helping other people accept your friend. By showing others your acceptance of your friend for what he/she is, others might be encouraged to do so.

7. Be careful not to impose your own values and likes upon your friend. This may be difficult, because whilst it is important to ascertain what his/her likes or dislikes are, many handicapped people may not have had opportunities to express themselves. Therefore give them opportunities to do so.

8. Try to find subjects in common with your friend as a basis for exchange of ideas.

9. Help your friend to understand the complex area of social skills, i.e. learning to listen to others and taking turns in conversation, allowing for other people's feelings, how to initiate approaches to other people.

This project is being independently evaluated by the Thomas Coram Institute of the University of London. The questions being addressed include the following: (i) What does the mentally handicapped person learn? (ii) What do the volunteers learn? (iii) What styles of interaction between the handicapped and normal students arise? (iv) Does the presence of mentally handicapped students affect the satisfaction and progress of volunteer students and other students in the class? (v) Do curriculum areas affect interaction? (vi) What are the more general effects in the Adult Education Institute?

We are conscious, as elsewhere in this chapter, that the examples selected could be multiplied many times over. Our concern however is to underline the importance of *alternatives* for intellectually disabled young people as they finally leave the statutory responsibility of the school system, within whatever administrative structure it may operate. The link between "school education" for them, whether provided separately in special schools or classes or in more integrated arrangements, and "adult", "continuing" or "further" education is vital. If *by definition* they are "very slow learners", it is obvious that suitable opportunities to go on learning *must* be provided—and without a break.

Educational use of television
Prior to late 1976, very few and limited attempts had been made anywhere in the world to make use of television as an educational medium for adults who were disabled by intellectual impairment. Within two years of a decision made at that date, the Continuing Education Department of the BBC launched its first series—twelve 12-minute programmes—for moderately intellectually disabled older children and adults, under the title *Let's Go*, and a year later a second series became available, as *Let's Go 2* (Croton, 1980). *Let's Go 3*, together with repeats of programmes from the first two series, is being launched in late 1982. This pioneering venture has attracted worldwide interest, and will undoubtedly stimulate national and regional efforts to produce indigenous programmes.

Systematic independent evaluation of the first two series showed that, as expected, some of the units were less successful across the board than were others; the target audience should be identified as men and women attending adult training or social education centres; additional viewing times suitable for their places of residence were essential, and that then close cooperation between day centre and home was both possible and highly desirable; and that the availability and use of video-recording equipment was a critical requirement if the full educational potential of the programmes was to be realized. It was also found, encouragingly, that the carefully-prepared *Notes* and slide-packs were highly valued by staff in the centres using the series.

At the decision point in early 1982 about the launching of *Let's Go 3* later that year, units from the two earlier series that seem likely to be repeated include "Let's . . . go shopping; and telephone; and get ready (to go out); and look after our teeth; and eat out." Topics (in some cases revised versions of old units) likely to appear in the new series include: looking after clothes; simple cooking; going on holiday; home safety; participation in decision-making.

A "significant life without work"

This phrase, one of very recent origin not only in the field of intellectual disablement, was used earlier when describing the work being done at the North Nottinghamshire College of Further Education. We must return to it before ending this section, if only in order to emphasize the word "significant" and its implications for service planners and providers. Those adults who are intellectually severely impaired, or whose multiple impairments constitute a major permanent disablement, have traditionally been left in the back wards of large institutions, and far too many are still there. If they live in their parental home, some have been found places in day service units such as so-called "adult training centres", "activity therapy centres", or "special care units".

For most of them there has never been any realistic expectation that they would in our work-oriented societies find a "significant life" through paid employment whether open or sheltered. But increasingly it is being recognized that many of their companions, less severely or multiply disabled, have little better prospects however much imaginative and sustained effort may be exerted on their behalf. In the technologically most advanced countries of the world, there is a growing awareness of the possibility that millions of ordinary adults without impairment will be denied, by a combination of social and economic forces, what has been regarded as a "human right"—to be employed, to "earn an adequate living". It is against that background that we must now build into our educational services—in school and after school—for intellectually impaired persons, a large element of training in *the positive use of daily living time*, so as to minimize the social and personal loss of "significance" in a life where paid employment cannot provide it.

It is at this point that one needs to take issue with the use being made of the word "work". Clearly it is almost always assumed to be synonymous with "paid employment", and in that usage we contrast it with "leisure" or "play". Here we ignore the physical and mental effort that many unimpaired people expend during their "leisure" time or when they "are at play". In fact "play" has been defined as "working hard at something you chose to do"; this is obvious in early childhood and is a key element in all good pre-school education.

An example of a positive approach to the problems of enforced leisure is provided by the PATH (Parents and their Handicapped Teenagers) project (Jeffree, 1979). This four-year action research project, based on the Hester Adrian Research Centre at the University of Manchester, is concerned with the leisure-time activities of very young adults. It was found, in the first stage of the study, that most of these severely intellectually disabled teenagers have a restricted circle of friends and a limited choice of activities. Most of their time was spend in passive, solitary "activities" such as listening to radio or records, or watching the television. In this they obviously do not differ sharply from their non-disabled peers, with whom however they had few contacts. Outings and other "occasions" were largely family oriented and initiated. The second stage of this project is concerned with exploring ways in which this limited pattern can be changed, and it is to be hoped that the findings will stimulate positive intervention elsewhere.

Another potentially valuable approach is to be found in the concept of voluntary service *by* intellectually disabled people. Dickson (1976) described how a very progressive adult training centre, in a rural setting three miles from the famous cathedral city of Salisbury in southern England, successfully approached two local organizations for elderly people. The result of the first invitation, for three trainees to visit a community centre for old people, where they would help with serving refreshments, was a string of requests for more such "teams". Later projects involved the local geriatric hospital, brass polishing in the cathedral, gardening for infirm elderly people living in their own homes and helping with physically handicapped children in the local hospital. The author (Dickson, 1976, p. 137) noted that:

> Their enthusiasm and developing sense of responsibility is obvious; it also provides opportunities for integration, communication, and putting into practice skills learned, and *above all the knowledge that each individual has something worthwhile to give, for which he is needed and valued. People even ask for his help.* (Our italics).

Finally, we should note the potential role of public libraries. In an official publication (Department of Education and Science, 1978b), it was made clear that libraries should be thinking of those who are barred from the normal use of libraries by a physical or mental handicap.

A Place to Live

Given that the parents or foster-parents are provided with adequate support, including easy-to-use and acceptable arrangements for short-term and emergency relief, we have recognized that all but a very few intellectually—or even multiply—impaired children should stay in the parental home. We must now turn, as has been necessary several times already, to the question of what happens when John or Mary reaches 18 or 21 and becomes an adult—physically and legally. There are three possibilities: they can stay where they are, they can be found a place in some public or private "residential setting", or they can be enabled to live as ordinary a life as possible out in the open community. Let us examine these in turn.

The parental home

In many countries these days, intellectually disabled adults do stay on in the parental home. If they are severely or multiply disabled, or if they become emotionally volatile or overactive and restless, their presence can create growing and often insoluble problems for the parents. But even without such complications, there is also the real possibility that their very slow learning processes will receive less and less stimulation, just when they need more—and of a different kind from that appropriate in childhood. Quite understandably their parents may unintentionally restrict their development and their progress towards independence. Necessary and reasonable risks may not be entertained. The great "plus" of living in a familiar caring environment can be overdone. And as the parents pass middle age, the question inevitably arises, "What will happen when we are no longer able to cope, or are no longer here?". In a survey carried out in 1976, one English county social services department found that three quarters of the families with an intellectually-disabled adult in the age-range 30–39 years had no plans for when the caregiver could no longer cope. In the neighbouring county of Devon, one-third of all the intellectually-disabled adults living at home had one or both parents aged 65 or over. In a recent small-scale intensive study (Wertheimer, 1981) it was found that older parents "rarely see themselves as having any part to play in planning the mentally handicapped person's future; nor does there seem to be any move to involve the mentally handicapped people themselves" (p. 33). The risk—and at present in most countries the reality—is that eventually most middle-aged adults living in the parental home will face a double bereavement: of one or both parents and of a long-familiar environment.

One systematic attempt to remove this "second bereavement" is represented by the creation in Britain of the MENCAP Homes Foundation. Among other possible funding arrangements it would enable parents to leave their house to the Society in return for a legal undertaking that the Society would continue to care for their intellectually disabled son or daughter, unless circumstances changed in such a way as to render this inappropriate. The operation of the scheme would in each local authority area require the prior agreement and cooperation of that authority, since it has the ultimate responsibility under the existing legislation.

The "residential setting"

If an adult, at any age, does leave the parental home, he or she is at present in many countries most likely to "have been found a place" by others, usually without consultation and often without even a preliminary familiarization visit. In what until very recently has been regarded as a modern highly-developed "service", such as that created in Sheffield during the 1970s, that "place" would be in some form of residential institution, whether relatively large (a hospital) or relatively small (a hostel). We have learned from the Sheffield evaluation studies that this represents a far from satisfactory solution in *practice*. There is a rapidly growing conviction that it is a wholly unsatisfactory solution in *principle*. Just as the appropriate place for an intellectually-impaired child is in the parental home, with adequate support and relief, or with foster-parents if that is a necessary alternative, so the appropriate place for him or her later as an adult is out in the ordinary community among ordinary people.

Community living

As is widely known, this principle was most fully pioneered in practice in Omaha, Nebraska, through the creation of the Eastern Nebraska Community Office of Retardation (ENCOR) in 1970. At that time, its community-based residential services were developed on the group-home model (6–8 persons), supplemented by specialized services. By 1975, it had been found that this approach presented many drawbacks—in the use of individual programmes, in movement of clients through the system, and in community acceptance of intellectually disabled persons. In 1975, it was decided to retain only six group homes for adults, and to develop the "Alternative Living Unit" (ALU) concept instead of establishing more group homes. An ALU is intended to serve three or fewer individuals, and its purpose is to meet the specific individual needs of each resident. Using a two-level structure—"regions" and "clusters"—for residential services and specialized services (including respite care), ENCOR is able to support each ALU as needed, to allow for internal client movement, and to supervise and monitor the overall individualized service. Ordinary houses are rented, not bought, and ALUs may be staffed on a "live-in" or on a shift basis. ENCOR works in close cooperation with the very active local parents association, the Greater Omaha Association for Retarded Citizens (GOARC) to which in fact it originally owed its creation. GOARC is strongly concerned to maintain the gains that have been achieved through ENCOR, and expresses this not only through cooperation, support, fund-raising and political lobbying, but also through constructive criticism of its work. In mid-1981 the Association had three monitoring teams in action, concerned with the quality of ENCOR's residential services, not least because economic pressures could threaten the very small 'ALUs on which these are based. GOARC is fully aware that services elsewhere in the United States, in Canada, and outside North America—such as Queensland in Australia—still look to the ENCOR model as one of the most acceptable bases for comprehensive community services.

Since 1975 the official policy of the Intellectual Handicap Branch of the Queensland State Health Department has been to develop an ALU system along ENCOR lines. Queensland went further than did Nebraska, by replacing all the nurses in its state institutions with "care workers" for whose training a new course was worked out in collaboration with a college of advanced education. (The nurses were absorbed into the mental illness services). Even with this positive move, the hospitals are regarded as a residual feature of an out-dated system. This view is certainly not accepted readily by most medical and nursing professionals, or by many health and social service administrators, simply because it is not credible to them. They argue that only a hospital can provide adequately for the needs of severely and/or multiply disabled adults, or for those displaying mental illness symptoms leading to disruptive or overactive behaviour. It seems to be a case of "only seeing is believing"; but let ENCOR at least indicate its response in the evocative words of a recent visitor from Britain (Libby, 1981, p. 6):

> An example of how ENCOR tries to serve the needs of clients was given. One man, aged 21, had been living with his parents and they were requesting residential help. This young adult was 6' tall, weighed 200 lbs and was said to hit people. They began by planning a residence just for

him with 24 hour staff cover on a shift system with no one member of staff living in the house. As his behaviour modified, staff began to live in and they were able to work with him by having a member of staff overnight and two staff present during waking time. As he further developed, other clients moved in to share the house with this person. Thus all the time the aim was to achieve a normal living situation and by very heavy staff input gradually being withdrawn this was achieved. This method of staff input gradually being reduced is a common one with ENCOR. The number of staffing hours needed is worked out as people's skills improve and their dependency lessens, so staff can be withdrawn and placed in new residences. It is thus, very importantly, that staff will be more frequently moved rather than clients.

The nub of the matter is that if—as in the planning of the Sheffield Development Project—you start with "the buildings you need", you come out with a fundamentally different attitude and action-pattern from what would result from starting with "what the individual needs". You also have to find a lot of capital funds for "purpose-built units", and enormous sums—forever—to maintain and staff them. All this expenditure must reduce the amount available for services provided to families and to individuals in the community.

In the MORC programme for adults there are two kinds of group home: the "contract group home" (CGH) and the "alternative intermediate service" (AIS), plus apartment accommodation in ordinary blocks in the community. In the case of CGHs, the "investor" leases the home to the state government; the "administrator" has a contract with MORC; and the state Department of Social Services licenses the home, monitoring its physical standards and quality of operation through MORC, as the "supervisory agency". Increasingly, the extension of this CGH approach is via "current ownership situations", MORC actively recruiting in the community for owners of suitable homes—who are themselves likely to be suitable as administrators. All potential CGH administrators are given a 12-weeks training by MORC professional staff: this is mostly "on-the-spot in-service", plus a small amount of "classroom time" mainly concerned with licensing requirements and procedural questions. During that period the potential administrator receives a 30 hours per week "stipend". Licensing of the CGH is provisional for six months; if satisfactory, the licence is extended to three years, and if still satisfactory it is then made permanent. MORC monitoring however continues indefinitely. Most CGHs accommodate 4 to 6 adults, but as clients whose needs are greater are being sought places, this figure is falling to 2 or 3.

A typical social worker "case manager" in the CGH part of the programme would be likely to have responsibility for five homes, with 6½ full-time-equivalent staff per home to give a cover of two staff at any one time, except at night and during the day Monday to Friday, when one is sufficient. The staff in each group home are employed by the administrator under the contract with MORC, as are the necessary supporting professionals (on a part-time or "sessional" basis). Individual programmes for residents are worked out and monitored in consultation with the MORC professional team. In addition to the weekly monitoring by the case-managers, the system as a whole is also under regular review by MORC's "Quality of Life Review Teams", and by the Parent Monitoring Committee. Of these two, the former are made up of two MORC staff members drawn from all sections of the agency *except* the Community Placement Programme. Four of these two-person teams visit an average of one CGH each month during their one-year spell of service.

The AIS (alternative intermediate service) residences were being operated in 1981 by MORC on an equal funding basis as between Federal and State agencies. These are intended for "severely limited and multiply handicapped adults" whom it is hoped can be enabled to progress to less restrictive community accommodation. The service is designated "intermediate" because most of the residents will come from a state institution. Because the residences have to meet strict guidelines laid down by the funding agencies, they tend to be purpose-built or heavily modified houses, and can therefore be roughly equated to small "hostels" in other systems.

In what MORC style the "whole-life program", which does not have to be state-licenced, adults live in apartments without resident staff or direct cover, but have a nearby "resource and training centre" which may serve more than one such complex and/or have other support responsibilities. In mid-1981 there were about twenty-five adults covered by this programme or (in two units) by Swedish-type arrangements within a single apartment building, with resident staff nearby.

Movement towards community living

Whatever may be their attractive features—and there are many—the ENCOR and MORC systems cannot be treated as "models" to be replicated elsewhere. They are challenging examples of what *can* be done; the philosophy is exportable, the structure may not be. The movement towards intellectually-disabled adults being enabled to live as independently as possible amongst their fellow citizens, in ordinary accommodation, has gained momentum from these major pioneering efforts. But now in each country, each administrative area has to work out its own way of realizing the philosophy in practice, right there in the realities of the national and local political and economic climate, and of general public attitudes.

During 1979, the King's Fund Centre in London convened a series of small workshops, to explore how local residential services which include aspects of the ENCOR model might be developed in Britain. This initiative resulted in the publication of a seminal project paper under the title *An Ordinary Life* (King's Fund Centre, 1980).

In this paper, a *residential service* "aims to provide a home and home-life for people who cannot find them independently. It makes it possible for people to live in a home of their own." To achieve this you need to find suitable ordinary *buildings*, and to provide *people* to "staff the service and bring to it their home-making skills. People who work as home-makers have two kinds of tasks—"doing" and "teaching" . . . they help their clients to provide for themselves what they need to make a home (and) teach their clients to be more independent in the business of independent living" (p. 12). The paper goes on to examine the components of a comprehensive community service; the problems and tasks involved in planning such a service; the varieties of potentially suitable housing and ways of obtaining it (without purchase wherever possible); the respective tasks of direct care staff and of managers; and local strategies for innovation.

Towards the end of the previous chapter, a very brief indication was given of how some of this was put into practice following the Sheffield evaluation and the actual recommendation of the Working Group on "living arrangements" was quoted (p. 84). Elsewhere in Britain local planning teams have been active, especially but not only where a fresh initiative was required if further progress of the right kind was to be made in getting people out of the long-stay hospitals. One reason for the timely value of the King's Fund paper is the growing evidence that the "exodus" frequently was *not* to properly-planned community residential services, but into "purpose-built" small hospitals and hostels of the very type found unsatisfactory in Sheffield. A notable example of a planned new start, however, comes from an inner urban area just south of the Thames, near London Bridge—the Guy's Health District. Like almost all areas in the metropolis, this one has traditionally depended on one of the very large institutions, about 30 miles away. When, as part of a comprehensive plan for services to be operated in close cooperation with the two relevant local authority social service departments, the planning team came to "residential services", it started effectively from zero so far as existing provision *within* the area was concerned. So the philosophy and service proposals and principles of *An Ordinary Life* were followed: use ordinary housing and develop the appropriate support services. This proposal was accepted.

Boarding-out

Another method, sometimes called "adult fostering" has been launched successfully in several places, including Leicestershire. This scheme originated in early 1979, when about twenty residents in a long-stay hospital were placed in the homes of eight landladies, with support from the Boarding-out Officer in the hospital. During the next twelve months the pressure for more places built up, not only from within the hospital but also from hostels, and from field social workers who were having difficulty in finding suitable accommodation for clients whose parental home situation had broken down. A limited newspaper advertising programme, backed up by posters and leaflets (delivered by volunteers to private houses in Leicester) was fairly successful, and by early 1982 sixty-eight intellectually disabled adults were living in the homes of twenty-four landladies.

All this was achieved by one Boarding-out Officer, who was eventually travelling about 1000 miles per month in her car, and frequently working extra unpaid hours during evenings and some weekends. Success clearly demanded additional staff resources. Apart from two sisters who ran what was in effect a large boarding house (rented from the local authority), with eighteen residents, most landladies (or married couples) took only one or two residents. The per capita payment made was £34 per week in 1981 figures. Considerable care is of course taken in assessing potential candidates for placement, with particular note being taken of any known incidents of violent behaviour. Here it is of interest to note that several of these private households have excelled in dealing with "difficult" adults coming from social service hostels. In addition to this boarding-out scheme, the health and local authority services also endeavour to place—with or without support—other adults capable of greater independent living in municipal flats and houses. Recently, in Sheffield, arrangements have been made between the housing and social services departments of the local authority for a system of "flexible letting". This enables the social services to place intellectually disabled adults in houses owned by the city, and to use such houses in a variety of ways: one large old house might for example be converted into a number of "bed-sitting-rooms", support being provided by visiting "home helps" as found to be necessary. One consequence of this development is a recognition by the adult training centres (where many of these "independent living" persons spend much of their weekday time) of the need for greater emphasis on the programmed teaching of self-care, domestic, inter-personal and social skills.

The older adult

As noted elsewhere, the proportion of intellectually disabled persons surviving into middle age and later life has been steadily increasing. Quite apart from the problems created by the death or incapacity of even older parents, where the disabled son or daughter has never left home, services are now faced with finding individually appropriate accommodation for those who have spent most of their lives in hostels, group homes or even semi-independently in the community. The scale of the problem for the parental-home group was recently illustrated by a Leicestershire survey. This showed that of the 529 adults living at home, 140 were with parents over sixty years of age, 101 of these being 60–69, 31 aged 70–79, and the remaining eight aged over 80 years.

Within the framework of an "ordinary life" philosophy, every service-providing agency will endeavour to keep to a minimum the number of elderly disabled people who end up in an institutional setting. The "adult fostering" approach may in itself provide a partial solution, as will a progressive increase in support, as needed, to those living in group homes or independently with one or two disabled companions. At present, for those for whom transfer to other accommodation becomes essential, the most frequently-adopted solution is the conventional "old people's home". This at least treats the intellectually disabled older person no differently from those who have lived a normal life, but have had the misfortune to reach later life no longer able to look after themselves, and either without relatives who can provide them with a home or for whom the task has become too demanding. Our aim must be to keep resort to this final solution at a minimum for *all* elderly people. This is, however, probably the appropriate place to note that evidence is accumulating to show an expected onset of pre-senile dementia in adults with Down's Syndrome at or soon after the age of 50 years.

Current developments in the Netherlands

As most of this section has been illustrated by examples drawn from the United States and Britain, it is important to record a recent spontaneous upsurge of interest among residential providers in the Netherlands. It will be recalled that under the Dutch system, all such provision is made through subsidy of private organizations. This includes everything on the residential front from large institutions to small hostel-type residences.

At the time of writing, the Bishop Bekkers Foundation is funding a nationwide study of the efforts being made in more than forty settings, to promote "community-integrated living" for intellectually disabled adults. (Opmeer, 1982, personal communication). Most of these spontaneous initiatives involve only those who are less severely disabled. But there are in addition at least two examples of a similar initiative for persons with greater degrees of dependency. One involves a large institution, a substantial section of which accommodates intellectually disabled persons, the remainder being for those who are mentally ill. For some years it has been intended that movement out into the community should take place, but it was felt that local attitudes were unprepared for anything like genuine integration. Recently, a decision was taken to build what in effect will be a new village, between the site of the big institution and the existing "old" village. The houses in the new village will be ordinary modern dwellings; in some of them intellectually disabled adults from the institution will be housed, while in others "friends of the disabled" will live. It is expected that this latter group will be recruited from three main sources: relatives of present residents in the institution, people who already work there (in any capacity), and people who are interested in living in such a novel "service" setting.

It is intended that residents in the large institution of "all severity levels" should be considered for placement in the new village, which is scheduled for first occupancy in 1985. The mixed community planning makes possible real independence from the institution, except for specialist professional services when needed. Each household will—with as much assistance as may be needed from the non-disabled neighbours—carry out its domestic work, do its own shopping, and cook its own meals. The institution has received government approval for the capital cost of the housing for the intellectually disabled residents in the first half of a two-stage plan for the new village, but the "green-light" to go ahead was (in mid-1982) not available for a subsidy required to enable the houses for non-disabled residents to be offered at reasonable rentals.

The other difficulty facing this imaginative scheme is however generalizable to the whole Dutch movement for community integration. Under the system described in Chapter 3 (p. 59) all *community* social workers are employees of the central ministry. Even if, as is planned, this is devolved to regions, the hard fact will still be that there are not enough social workers to make it likely that they will be able to cope with supporting a new set of clients. The solution would seem to lie in the institutions individually accepting responsibility for the support of their residents when no longer "within the walls". But at this point fresh problems arise, both from the fact that national funding of institutions is separate, as noted earlier, and from the conservative attitudes of many directors on their powerful boards.

The second example involves a quite small institution (100 residents) in a different part of the country. Some time go, when extensive repairs and alterations were seen to be needed soon, it was realized that a temporary accommodation problem for some of the residents could be solved by renting four houses in a nearby small town. The opportunity was taken to carry out an "action experiment", using before-and-after assessment of the persons involved (over a period of ten months), and a survey comparison of attitudes at the *end* of this period, between neighbours of the four rented houses towards "mentally retarded people", and residents in another strictly comparable part of the same town. The results are positive on both counts; the disabled people have improved significantly on such measures as "self-care", "social contact skills" and "incidence of disruptive behaviour"; and the attitudes of the neighbours were found to be more positive than were those of the sample of residents in the other part of the town. As a result, although the renovation work at the institution has been completed, those who spent the ten months in the four rented houses asked to stay—and this has been agreed. It remains to be seen what the longer-term implications of this experiment will be, not only for that small institution but elsewhere in the Netherlands. The same can of course be said about the "new village" venture.

Purpose-built accommodation

In the example just cited of a Dutch initiative, a large institution plans to build some new accommodation: ordinary modern houses *outside*, in a "new village". Some large long-stay hospitals and institutions in

Australia, Britain and North America have in recent years built "villas" or even small houses *inside* their own estates. In Britain, at least, many health and local authorities are still planning and building "hostels", most often to "accommodate in as home-like a setting as possible" 24 adults who are either not considered likely to "succeed" in unstaffed group homes in the community, or for whom no such accommodation is likely to be provided in that particular area. During the last ten years or so, a few architects have specialized in this kind of design work, and a growing amount of ingenuity has been displayed. For example, the new 96-bed "small hospital units" in Sheffield consist of four 24-bed blocks, each internally split into two sections. Similarly, the new 24-place hostels, both for health service and local authority residents, are internally subdivided—or ranged across the site. The human implications for both staff and residents of all these various attempts to make mini-institutions more "home-like" have been carefully evaluated by members of the Mental Health Buildings Evaluation Programme, in the DHSS Works Group, London. Ten reports (DHSS) have been published on the Sheffield buildings, old and new.

Four checklists were used: the Index of Community Involvement (ICI); the Index of the Physical Environment (IPE); the Revised Resident Management Practices scale (RRMP)—all of which are in Raynes, Pratt and Roses (1979)—and The 39 Steps (Gunzburg, 1973). The authors of the DHSS reports note that all of these have limitations, but taken together can be used to indicate a consistent trend, towards or away from the "institutional".

In Report S8, on adult residential accommodation (DHSS, 1981), the principal finding was that smaller units achieved *better* scores on all four checklists, yet were if anything *less expensive*. So if anyone, anywhere, is compelled to design a "purpose-built unit of accommodation" for intellectually disabled adults, instead of an ordinary dwelling, the smaller they are the better—where "better" means "more nearly ordinary" *and* "not more expensive". They will be better still if they are not made to look unusual—or even institutional—by being clustered together, complete with single entrance-way and parking space for staff cars.

Roles for Voluntary Service

Whatever may be the philosophy, structure and operational style of the services provided for intellectually disabled children and adults, there

must always be a place for the unpaid contributions of ordinary
people. We should like at this point to get inside the conventional
grouping styled "the voluntary sector". It already has identifiable
components familiar to most readers; but other and wider roles have
been developing in recent years to which attention must be drawn.

Parent action and reaction

Locally, nationally, and internationally the contribution made by
groups of parents of intellectual disabled children and adults has
been—and remains—predominant. That must not however be taken
to mean that the majority of parents are actively involved in the work
of the organization of which they are members. All too often there is
good reason for their apparent lack of involvement; they are left
without either time or energy to make an active contribution simply
by the unrelenting demands of the home situation. In fact, one is
frequently amazed by what some parents *do* somehow manage to give
to the general "cause", through their local or national society. Like
everything else, the situation varies widely from one place to another,
and from one time to another within a single community.

It is obvious that the steady trend in many countries to reduce the
placement of children in long-stay institutions—in some places to near
zero, even where profound impairment is involved—will have laid an
increasing burden on the home. As has already been observed,
home-support services and short-term care facilities have failed to
keep pace with this trend. Voluntary activity on the part of parents of
intellectually disabled adults living at home, instead of being away in
an institution, has also been curtailed despite improvements in local
day-provision of one kind or another. The problem is especially acute,
as we have already noted, when overactivity and emotional problems
add significantly to the domestic strain.

We do not, therefore, find it at all surprising that some parents'
organizations eventually tend towards a conservative philosophy.
Where only a minority of the paid-up members feel able to take an
active role, or to serve as officers or on management committees, there
must be a risk of that occurring. The spread of "new ideas"—even if
far from new elsewhere—about intellectually disabled adults moving
out of the family home into some form or other of residence in the
ordinary community, can be alarmingly radical to many older
parents. Their voluntary efforts may to them seem best applied to the
promotion of schemes which are intended to guarantee protective
care, after they are no longer able to provide it themselves. The issue

of parental misgivings about community placement for their adult offspring has recently been considered by the placement coordinator and the director of MORC (Rosenau and Provencal, 1981) in a searching and constructive paper, based on their own experience in the Macomb Oakland area of moving over 700 disabled people from state institutions to small group homes, apartments, foster homes, or similar "normative" living accommodation in the community. They enunciate five basic operating principles for the agency, each of which we illustrate by a short quotation.

1. *From the beginning: respect*

A mother concerned about the safety of her 42-year-old son being considered for a group home should not be answered by a scolding sermon on the "dignity of risk".

2. *Know and show where the buck stops*

Parents must know that the agency's responsibility exists whether they are in the picture or not.

3. *Making a house a home*

The new home must appear immediately as an appealing place to live . . . generic support service . . . should be accessible and of high integrity.

4. *A guide through the labyrinth*

It is essential for the placement coordinator to feel personally involved with the transfer from the institution to the community.

5. *A stitch in time*

. . . families who are new to the system should be acquainted with the preference of community rather than institutional living . . . parents and guardians with established institutional relationships should be introduced to this preference *today*.

Rosenau and Provencal then suggest "ten linear steps" through which the parent or guardian can be guided, in order to develop a practical understanding of, and confidence in, the placement. These we simply list:

    1. Visit a community placement
    2. Visit the proposed home
    3. Meet the person in charge
    4. Observe the home's direct service
    5. Meet the monitoring social worker

6. Visit the day programme
7. Meet the interdisciplinary team

If at this point they remain unconvinced, three more "experiences" are recommended:

8. Meet other parents/guardians (alone or in parent groups)
9. Meet senior responsible officers in the placing agency
10. Meet an unbiased client advocate, e.g. from the local Association

This intensely practical article is "required reading" for everyone who participates in the community placement of intellectually disabled persons.

Citizen advocacy

While the idea of "speaking on behalf of another person" is certainly not new, either in the legal setting or in everyday life, it is less than a decade since the foundations were laid for an advocacy movement in relation to intellectually disabled persons (Wolfensberger and Zauha, 1973). Two years later John O'Brien was involved from the outset with what became the Georgia Advocacy Office, and the Canadian Association for the Mentally Retarded published a comprehensive and closely-reasoned monograph (Wolfensberger, 1977). But quite possibly the first pioneers were two parents, Katie Dolan and Janet Taggart, who in mid-1972 made an agreement with the North-west Centre for the Retarded in Seattle, to develop a manual on "how to get benefits for disabled adults". The office expenses were to be covered by a $12500 per annum grant from the regional office of the federal Department of Health, Education and Welfare, and the two parents worked on a voluntary basis. Within a month, they were so appalled by the problems in the "system" that they decided to start helping families individually, and to work on the system at the same time. In this way the agency known as *The Troubleshooters* came into being; by 1977 the state governor made it "the designated Protection and Advocacy Agency throughout the state (Washington) for all persons with developmental disabilities and other handicaps". The main aim of Katie Dolan, since 1976 the full-time director, is to help the family, the parent, the disabled person to "grow into self-advocacy"—by learning how to use the system. But *The Troubleshooters* retain the advocacy responsibility as long as and to the extent that it is needed by the client.

Citizen advocacy on the O'Brien/Wolfensberger model, as developed in Georgia and in Canada, is by contrast a long-term one-to-one "matching" between the disabled person and the advocate recruited and trained by the agency. In this model, citizen advocacy involves a competent citizen, unpaid, who creates a relationship with a disabled person, and chooses one or more of many possible roles to understand, respond to and represent that person's interests as if they were his or her own. It is emphasized that adequate acceptance of such a role will always imply a distinct *cost* to the advocate. Wolfensberger (1977) spells this out (p. 20).

> This distinct cost may involve any number of things: time that one would much rather have spent on something else; wear and tear on one's emotions, such as one would ordinarily avoid; investment of one's material substance and possessions; sacrifice of rest, sleep and/or recreation, etc. . . . Indeed, without significant cost, an action should not be viewed as advocacy . . .

He—and everyone involved in the citizen advocacy movement—warns against the insidious danger inherent in "conflict of interest". Not only must the individual advocates and the recruiting agencies be wholly (and visibly) independent of the service-delivering persons, agencies and institutions, but acceptance of public funds by the independent advocacy agency must be on an explicitly untied basis.

Against this background, it is not at all surprising that by 1977 it was already possible to detect a sobering trend in the performance of the more than two hundred citizen advocacy agencies that had sprung up in the wake of the 1975 US Federal Developmental Disabilities Act (Wolfensberger, 1977, p. 40).

> There has been a tendency to assign advocates to the more "interesting", more verbal, more affectionate and lovable people in need. In consequence the pool of potential advocates was often drained of those who might have taken on the interests of persons who may have needed advocacy the most: those who are non-communicative, profoundly impaired, unattractive for some reason, institutionalized, totally abandoned, etc.

It is therefore of perhaps special interest to consider the structure and approach of the first organized approach to this question in the United Kingdom, which did not occur until 1981. Following a substantial period of informal discussion, five national charitable organizations—including the two representing the mentally ill and the intellectually disabled—formed a new body known as *The Advocacy Alliance*. By early 1982, enough progress had been made to cover an initial annual budget of £110 000, to which a contribution of £40 000, spread over three years, is being made by the national government's Department of Health and Social Security. The Alliance is fully satisfied that this government contribution in no way affects its complete independence.

Initially, the approach will be to long-stay NHS institutions for adults, and with a focus on residents without relatives (or who never visit them). Discussions will be initiated, one or two hospitals at a time, with the staff and administrative officers. If and when full agreement is reached, the Advocacy Alliance will seek to recruit, and then to train, local volunteers as advocates on a one-to-one basis. With one large hospital already prepared to cooperate and a second agreeing in principle, the target in early 1982 was to have sixty trained volunteer advocates in action by the end of that year. The first stage of the project is being evaluated by an independent team financed by a charitable trust. If all goes well, the long-term aim is to create a national network, and eventually to extend activities into the community-based residential services. Clearly, it is intended that this characteristically British "softly, softly", slow-but-sure strategy will develop and then keep pace with the national trend towards community living and local, community-based service provision. To the extent that it is successful, it will not only meet the advocacy needs of some of those "forgotten people", but will also encourage and stimulate other forms of voluntary activity on behalf of intellectually disabled persons.

Passing reference has been made to "self-advocacy" and to the ways in which the citizen advocate can help the intellectually-disabled person to "use the system". It has until very recently been assumed, tacitly or explicitly, that such members of our society cannot speak for themselves. This assumption is itself handicapping, and in the next section reference will be made to some successful efforts to counter it.

Self-advocacy

But for the timely appearance of a much-needed book (Williams and Shoultz, 1982), it would have been necessary to devote several pages to this topic. As it is, attention can be directed to salient features of this movement which apparently originated with conferences for intellectually disabled people in Sweden in the late 1960s. Such conferences soon took place in Britain (Shearer, 1972); in 1973 in British Columbia; in Oregon in 1974; and in Omaha, Nebraska, in 1975. As observed by Williams and Shoultz, the network of groups that sprang up in the United States during the 1970s included many that started as "independent local initiatives whose participants only later came to learn that they were part of a 'self-advocacy movement' " (Williams and

Shoultz, 1982, p. 56). They also note that similar groups can be traced back to the 1950s, though for long unrecognized.

The Oregon groups adopted the title "People First", and this by 1980 led to a two-day convention of People First International, attended by over 1000 people from all over the USA and Canada. Also in 1980, "United Together" came into being, at a national conference which also included representatives from self-advocacy groups of people disabled by cerebral palsy and epilepsy. Williams and Shoultz suggest (p. 60) that "a cooperative partnership between United Together and the People First movement is likely to be the foundation for increasing the strength of the self-advocacy movement in future years". They also note that, by 1979, one in six of the delegates to the annual conference of the Canadian Association for the Mentally Retarded (CAMR) were intellectually disabled themselves.

While in North America the trend has been strongly towards the formation of local groups in which intellectually disabled persons are enabled to assume leadership responsibilities, with a progressive reduction in the active role of their non-disabled advisers, the development in Britain has been of a different kind. According to Williams and Shoultz, the conferences and other events since the initial gathering in 1972 have become more and more "participation events" in which what Paul Williams had called "our mutual handicap" can be reduced (p. 166):

> Mentally handicapped people have a welcome chance to express themselves and to share activities with non-handicapped people, while (the latter) have the unusual chance, sometimes approached with trepidation, to share their lives for a short time on an equal basis with mentally handicapped people.

He goes on to express the hope, however, that this valuable development will in the near future be complemented by a revival of self-advocacy gatherings, as far as possible organized by intellectually disabled people.

Over recent years about one-fifth of the adult training centres in England and Wales have formed "trainee committees" or "student councils", which vary greatly in their mode of operation. Williams and Shoultz consider at length the current problems facing these bodies—identifying them as "inward-looking agendas, conflict of interest in the staff who help or belong to committees, and poor contact between committees and the trainees they represent" (p. 177). They therefore perceive most of them as "support groups" which are however laying part of a firm foundation for the development of a genuine self-advocacy movement in Britain. The other part could be provided by recognition of the need for self-advocacy within the very large number of leisure clubs—the majority run by local MENCAP societies, and therefore affiliated to a national federation. Only seldom do the intellectually disabled members find themselves on the organizing committee, and we are in full agreement with Williams and Shoultz when they say (p. 181):

> Within these clubs there are many opportunities offered for individual self-advocacy, and there is enormous potential for development of a self-advocacy role by the groups; but there is a general lack of awareness of what self-advocacy is or of its potential. Some of the perceptions of mentally handicapped people by the organising committees and by non-handicapped volunteers in the clubs would need to be modified if true self-advocacy were to be pursued. They would need to regard themselves more in the role of self-advocacy advisers. . . . Much greater involvement of mentally handicapped people themselves in the organisation and management of the clubs is required as a first step in the direction of self-advocacy.

Before leaving this topic, there are three points dealt with by Williams and Shoultz which we believe need to be emphasized. First, one of the natural tasks of the citizen advocacy movement is to promote and assist the development of the self-advocacy movement, at local, national and international levels. Second, there are two stages in self-advocacy. At the beginning, the members of the new group are naturally and properly concerned with their *own* needs; when they have gained skill and confidence and developed their own leadership, the members must move on to speak and act on behalf of *others*. Third, groups may have to be started by those whose intellectual impairment is less severe, and who possess some communication skills; but progressively those members with more severe impairment should be—and can be—*enabled* to take their share. This is a very important asset in the "battle against handicap".

Paradoxically, perhaps, there seems to be more general participation by parents where the system by which needs are met requires a service input from the "voluntary sector". Parents quite understandably become very identified with the school, the training centre, the sheltered workshop, the hostel, that *their* society has provided and manages—even though there is a "public sector" subsidy or contract to meet the running costs. So while one may be convinced that it is the *duty* of the state (or municipality) to provide the services—educational, health, social, vocational—needed by its intellectually disabled citi-

zens, it may be wise to recognize the potentially differing consequences of various ways by which that duty can be carried out
satisfactorily. A voluntary involvement on the part of parents which
does not lay upon them additional burdens is something which
is—quite literally—"worth scheming for".

Influencing the public

Important as is the task of concerned professionals in this context, the
major effort must come from the voluntary bodies and their members.
Once there is some degree of acceptance by them that the right place
for *all* intellectually disabled children and adults is *among us*—yes, even
if "hospital-type care" is provided on a 1 : 1 staffing basis in ordinary
houses—then the No. 1 target for "recruitment to support" becomes
friendly, understanding neighbours, followed closely by shop assistants,
police officers, bus conductors—and the general public. To their
accepted and legitimate role as pressure groups for more and better
services, the members—not just the officers—of the voluntary bodies
are now called upon to add "gentle persuaders". The time is past for a
primarily inward-oriented programme of activities; minimizing the
potential handicap of the intellectually impaired people for whom they
are concerned depends largely on a change towards *outward*-oriented
activities. New roles are waiting.

The Question of Standards

During the last decade increasing concern has been expressed in many
countries about the unsatisfactory provisions available to ensure that
the quality of services to intellectually disabled persons is at least as
good as the available resources permit. Here it is at once necessary to
define some terms which are frequently and confusingly used as if they
were synonymous.

The term "accountability" should be applied to any process which
ensures that resources are used for the purpose for which they were
intended. "Monitoring" can describe the activity of a service-delivering agency when internal procedures are set up to ensure that an agreed
policy is followed along lines approved by responsible management.
This leaves the term "evaluation" available for use when an independent study is made of a particular way of organizing and delivering a
service. (To assist in its continuing availability for this purpose, it
would be helpful if the term *"assessment"* was used when *individual*
characteristics or skills are at issue, rather than "evaluation").

Unfortunately there is abundant evidence that monitoring is conspicuous by its absence in far too many service agencies, whether
public or voluntary, in the field of intellectual disability. In the public
sector, the mechanisms may well exist, but their use is frequently
perfunctory and ineffectual. All too often the difficulty is fundamental
rather than a matter of practice, because objectives have never been
precisely defined and agreed criteria laid down against which progress
or the lack of it can be compared. We have seen this to characterize the
Sheffield Development Project, and can note here with satisfaction
that under the new strategic plan this matter has been explicitly
emphasized and spelled out in detail. It is now the responsibility of the
joint management to define objectives and obtain agreement on
appropriate criteria.

In the absence, or ineffective use for whatever reasons, of internal
monitoring it usually requires a public scandal or—unusually—an
independent evaluation to reveal the weaknesses in any service setting,
whether institutionally or community based. Unhappily, the all-too-
frequent scandals about long-stay institutions continue in many
countries simply to underscore the fact that it is not only the residents
("inmates", "patients") who are institutionalized—so are the staff.
Add to that the usual circumstance that staffing ratios are seriously
inadequate, even though *per capita* costs in long-stay institutions are
high, and the magnitude of the task defies solution.

But "de-institutionalization" must not be done too quickly, or the
results will be almost equally serious. So those responsible for
long-term planning must use short-term measures as an essential part
of it. Meanwhile scarce financial resources have to be divided between
two needs: to make the old institutions less institutional for the
remainder of the time they will be needed, and to initiate the
progressive development of well-coordinated community services of
the kinds we have been considering. Both old and new service systems
need evaluation in addition to internal monitoring. Evaluation can be
descriptive, normative or formative; of necessity, that carried out
uniquely in Sheffield was primarily descriptive. The best known
evaluation "package" which is explicitly normative is PASS—"Programme Analysis of Service Systems" (Wolfensberger and Glenn,
1975), based on the principles of "normalization" and "the least
restrictive alternative". An example of formative evaluation currently
in progress is built into the service pilot project known as NIMROD
in South Wales.

The necessity to use descriptive evaluation can fairly be said to provide *a priori* evidence that a system of service delivery is lacking in an important respect; it is neither explicitly based on an attempt to realize a definable quality or character of service, nor to attain clearly defined objectives for which criteria may be agreed without undue difficulty. The normative approach brings with it from "outside" an explicit philosophy, complete with techniques for establishing how far an actual service is performing consistently with that particular philosophy. A formative evaluation, as is implied by the term, is "in at the planning stage" of a new service—or of a new way of providing an existing service—so that detailed objectives may be identified and made explicit, and criteria devised in advance through discussion with the service providers themselves. This exercise will be carried out with the minimum of potential stress to all concerned, if a basic underlying philosophy has been worked out and accepted by those responsible for planning and launching the new service.

A thoughtful review of the PASS technique was carried out by Kuh (1978) with the primary object of considering whether it was a suitable tool for the health and social services in Britain. She makes it clear that although PASS measures quality of care against three separate criteria —the "principle of normalization", other service "ideologies", and "recognized administrative practices"—the first of these accounts for three-quarters of the total score in the evaluation of quality. Kuh goes on to explain in fair detail how the technique breaks down the "principles" into 50 operational concepts known as ratings, each of which has between three and six levels, each carrying a weight or score. These are summed to a total, which ranges from a maximum of +1000 through zero (minimal acceptable performance) to a minimum of −947.

Around +700 points represents "expected performance", but Kuh reports that the mean score for 100 evaluations under PASS III (during the period 1975–1977) was +229, "signifying an average level of attainment only modestly above the minimal acceptable".

PASS raters have been described in a training workshop by Wolfensberger as "persons with prior human service sophistication and with extensive training in the principle of normalization and the PASS technique. In order to use PASS validly, they must have studied certain materials, participated in a workshop and practicum lasting at least five days, and conducted a number of assessments under the guidance of more advanced raters". From all accounts he should have added that raters require a considerable amount of physical and psychological stamina, to survive both the training procedures and the "conciliation process" in which all the raters in a PASS evaluation *must agree*—even if, as is not unusual, this takes all night.

There can be no reasonable doubt that PASS III is currently the most comprehensive and rigorous evaluation procedure available for the quality of care in a service-providing setting, provided the principles of normalization are fully accepted as the primary, almost the only, source of criteria. We agree however, with Kuh in her expression of regret that—at the time of writing in early 1978—insufficient independent research had been done on either the reliability (test/retest) of the procedure, or into its effectiveness as a tool for change. The latter could not of course be measured satisfactorily until evidence on the former is available. This question received attention from Flynn in an edited volume (Flynn and Nitsch, 1980), entirely devoted to the application of the "normalization principle", including well over 200 references to the English-language literature on this topic. In a substantial section on PASS inter-rater reliability and internal consistency, Flynn has this to report:

> . . . in order to derive estimates of inter-rater reliability for the full PASS instrument, it was necessary to have recourse to a separate sample of PASS evaluation made by experienced raters whose individual ratings (and not merely team-conciliated ratings) were available. This independent inter-rater reliability sample (analysed in Flynn and Heal, 1980) consisted of 14 residential programs administered by the same agency in a Midwestern US city. For two reasons—similarity of program type, and administration by a single agency—the 14 residential programs were somewhat more homogeneous than a "typical" (unselected) sample would probably be. For this reason, the inter-rater reliability coefficients are probably somewhat lower than those that would be obtained from a more heterogeneous sample. . . . For the 50-item PASS scale, the inter-rater reliability coefficient (which is an intraclass generalizability coefficient, with rater bias included as part of the error term) for a *single* rater was found to be 0.704. This coefficient is the estimate of the average agreement between one rater and another in the (three-rater) PASS team that carried out the 14 residential assessments. The reliability (generalizability) of the average (mean) of the *three* raters' total PASS scores was found to be 0.877. Moreover, the mean of the three raters' total scores correlated very highly with the team's conciliated total PASS score (intraclass correlation = 0.933; Pearson correlation = 0.968) . . .

Wisely, Flynn injects a note of caution at this point, saying (parenthetically) that "obviously more generalizability studies on PASS need to be conducted, in which not only inter-rater but interteam reliability coefficients are estimated" (p. 336), which he reinforces later in the book (p. 390) by observing that "Many important issues such as interteam reliability, leniency errors, halo effects, and convergent and discriminant validity all need intensive study".

NIMROD is intended to be a demonstration project which could set the pattern for future comprehensive services. It arose from the report of a joint working party in 1978, and involves the close collaboration of the District Health Authority, the South Glamorgan County Council, the Cardiff City Council and the Welsh Office (the locus of United Kingdom central government in Wales). The project is planned over a seven-year period, during which financial responsibility for the services to a population of 60 000 will be gradually transferred from the Welsh Office and the health service to the County Council. Under a project coordinator there will be a staff of about fifty, spread across four "communities" each with its own "community care manager". It was estimated that there were upwards of 220 intellectually disabled persons to be served, of whom 55 had been identified as living in "mental handicap hospitals".

Details of this imaginative scheme have been published (Mathieson and Blunden, 1980) and are also set out more fully in the working party report (Welsh Office, 1978). For our present purpose, the additional significant element is the role of the Mental Handicap Wales Applied Research Unit, of which Roger Blunden is director. This will involve

> . . . developing, documenting and evaluating that service. During the preliminary phase of the project, research resources will be concentrated on the development of components of the service, and of the evaluative methods to be used. A number of measures will be taken at regular intervals throughout the project, showing quality and quantity of services delivered, and their impact upon clients, relatives and staff. By the end of the project reports will have been produced describing the service, the way in which it was implemented and the effects of its introduction (*op cit.* 1978, p. 13)

It is essential to appreciate that "the researchers are involved in the detailed design of the service, and will subsequently evaluate the effects of its implementation" (Mathieson and Blunden, 1980, p. 124). In other words, "formative" evaluation was *part* of the agreed plan for the project in advance.

In the context of a symposium on service evaluation, one of us (Heron, 1981) expressed the view that the future of programme evaluation in the field of intellectual disability lay in this "formative" paradigm in which evaluators work *from the outset* with planners, administrators and those responsible for actually providing the services. It was however noted (p. 415) that

> . . . acceptable standards of rigour and objectivity could only be achieved within such a paradigm through a high degree of specificity in both "goal" and "critical factor" identification, combined with equally specific "measures of outcome" for the individual client in a real-life context.

To this should be added the necessity for an accepted stated philosophy of service: as with the new Sheffield strategic plan, NIMROD has such a basis.

Conclusion

In this chapter we have endeavoured to show, mainly by the provision of examples, that through the well-planned combined efforts of the public and voluntary sources of services, the needs of intellectually disabled children and adults *can* be met by non-institutional strategies. The first requirement for progress in this way is an abandonment of the notion that such persons are "chronically sick". The second is a recognition of the essential need to relieve parents and relatives of the burden of care, through providing support, advice and respite—right from the start. The third is to convince the general public that the intellectually disabled person, appropriately supported in relation to his or her disabilities, can and should be fully accepted as a neighbour in the open community. The fourth is to raise and then to maintain standards, by internal systems of monitoring which are related to agreed objectives and agreed criteria, on the basis of an agreed philosophy of service. And finally, to learn as much as possible as quickly as possible from any and every innovative attempt to do better, through building formative evaluation into the plan and into its implementation.

We think it salutary to recall the variety of political and administrative systems described in Chapter 2. If necessary, systems can be altered in the interests of the individuals which they were created to serve. This will prove easier in some places and at some times than in others. It is our hope that the evidence made available here will aid and encourage those who are faced with the need to achieve such change.

CHAPTER 6

Starting From Nothing: The Third World

During the International Year of Disabled Persons (IYDP) in 1981, the United Nations IYDP Secretariat convened in Vienna a *World symposium of experts on technical cooperation among developing countries, and technical assistance in the field of disability prevention and rehabilitation.* As with most meetings and publications during the IYDP, the major bulk of the advance working papers for this symposium was concerned with physical disablement. This was strikingly consistent with the preliminary analysis of responses to the questionnaire sent by the IYDP Secretariat to all UN member countries:

> There is a clear indication that in all countries, mentally handicapped persons, and especially the severely handicapped adults, are given the lowest priority in most rehabilitation programmes.

In another working paper it was estimated that

> approximately 30–40 million mentally retarded persons are in need of daily assistance on a regular basis.

In this short volume, we have so far drawn our examples of strategies and systems for attempting to meet the needs of intellectually disabled children and adults—and their parents and relatives—from the "better-off" countries of the world. If we take together the two quotations above, it becomes unthinkable to shirk giving attention to the problems of that large majority of countries, accounting for 80% of this planet's human population, which make up what has been called "the Third World". If "in all countries mentally handicapped persons . . . are given the lowest priority . . .", then what must be the condition and prospects of those who are born intellectually impaired in countries where poverty for most inhabitants is endemic?

There are few general statements that can legitimately be made in answer to that question. It is of course true that in countries with high

153

infant mortality rates and a low expectation of life, fewer children born with severe intellectual impairment will survive into adulthood. For those who do, and more especially for those without additional physical disabilities who live in rural areas, there may be reasonable opportunity to live a "normal life". The probability of this occurring will depend in most cultures—as in fact it does in those of the "old World" and of the "New World" in the northern hemisphere—on the personal qualities and social behaviour of the individual. As Edgerton (1981, p. 314) has put it forcefully:

> . . . we need only note that virtually every study of mentally retarded persons has concluded that attitudes or "personality" attributes are more important in determining adaptive success than is intelligence as such. If we have not taken seriously the findings of research in our own society, then perhaps we can learn to heed what our "primitive" contemporaries tell us, namely, a person's intelligence matters, but his personal qualities matter even more.

There is another way in which the prospects for an intellectually disabled child or adult may be affected differentially from one culture (or subculture) to another. If to the confusion with mental illness is added a social conviction that no development or "improvement" is possible, then irrational fear and prejudice may characterize the public attitude. Tolerance for any apparent deviation from what is regarded as "normal" behaviour will be low. Once again, the similarity between many of the so-called "developed countries" and those in the Third World can be striking.

Gunnar Dybwad (1970) when commenting on an earlier paper by Edgerton, published in the same volume of conference proceedings, summed this up (p. 571):

> Edgerton believes, and I think correctly so, that any social system can make behaviour into a social problem. And I also agree with him that in determining societal differences we have been too concerned with environmental factors and the degree of technological achievement and, due to this preoccupation, have paid insufficient attention to more subtle qualities in the life of a nation or tribe, which would help us to understand why the citizens on developing Truk Islands and those in highly developed Denmark both have a far more positive and generous attitude towards the mentally retarded than countries in a similar developmental stage.

It therefore behoves us to approach the problem of unmet needs among the millions of intellectually disabled people in the Third World with a necessary caution and humility. This is not—just for once—a problem to which the export of technological expertise and equipment is very relevant. If it is possible—and as we shall see, it may not be for very practical rather than ideological reasons—for planners and providers in heavily-populated poor countries to avoid the institutionalization from which the wealthy ones are trying to extricate themselves, let us by all means help them to do so. But, by the same token, if any of them have hard-learned lessons to teach us, let us by all means be ready to listen.

Point of Departure

The prevalence of severe intellectual impairment in most Third World countries is not known. It can only be established by carefully-designed epidemiological surveys, appropriate in each case to the prevailing cultural, political and economic realities. Even if adequate resources were to be made available for such fact-finding activities, ethical considerations arise where the probability of even minimal preventative or therapeutic intervention is obviously very low. Given the understandable absence of handicap resulting from intellectual impairment from the priority lists of governmental and other agencies in these countries, it is not surprising that the first major initiative had to come from outside the Third World, or that this is a very recent event.

This initiative was taken by Sandor Németh, Director of the Bishop Bekkers Institute (BBI) in Utrecht, The Netherlands. Since its establishment in 1973, the BBI has promoted research on intellectual impairment and its consequences, and on the organization and delivery of services to meet them. In early May 1980 the Institute sponsored a "Workshop on the epidemiology of severe mental retardation" with particular emphasis on the developing countries. Much of what follows in this section of the chapter is based on—or quotes from—the issue of the International Journal of Mental Health containing the papers prepared for that workshop (Belmont, 1981). The workshop produced the following recommendations:

1. Epidemiological studies should be carried out to ascertain the prevalence of severe mental retardation in developing countries.

2. The target group should be *children* in the age-range *four to eight years*.

3. Variability in the prevalence of severe mental retardation, from place to place and group to group, should be examined and used in planning and prevention.

4. The epidemiological studies should use, as far as possible, a systematic and standard method of case identification.

5. In each region of the World Health Organisation (WHO) and also in each country, resource person(s) should be identified with special interest and experience in the field of mental retardation.

6. The screening and diagnostic instruments should be suitable for adaptation to use in ongoing primary health care units, especially in those that have access to referral centres.

These recommendations aroused the interest of several international bodies including WHO, UNICEF and Rehabilitation International. Practical implementation was initiated without delay, in particular the development of a screening device by two workshop participants, Lilian Belmont and Ann Clarke. By the end of 1980 this was being used in pilot form in ten countries, and its further development continues following a second meeting of most workshop members in Bangalore, in May 1981.

The discussions of the original workshop were lucidly summarized by Mittler (in Belmont, 1981, pp. 107–116). Having noted the grounds for optimism, afforded by the workshop material and discussion, about the growth of services for intellectually impaired children in developing countries, he goes on to direct attention to the grounds for concern (p. 114):

> Knowledge is one thing, implementation another. The gap between what we know and what we do is already far too wide. The economic situation is deteriorating in developed and developing countries alike. Even countries that have made significant advances in service delivery for handicapped people are now worried about the effect of the current economic recession on these services. Developing countries faced with problems of ill-health and poverty on a scale unknown in the West may be tempted to regard the problems of handicapped persons as a relatively low priority. From an organisational point of view, central governments often have little direct power to influence services for handicapped people; these are matters for local decision-making and local priorities.

This question of realistic tactics has increasingly pre-occupied those responsible for programme planning and funding in all the United Nations agencies. One of us (Heron, 1979) has explored the problem in the context of planning early childhood care and education (ECCE) services in developing countries, and this approach has subsequently been found useful by a WHO working party concerned with day care for the very young children of working mothers. Starting with the premise that "if any government in any country wishes to initiate, reform or extend ECCE provisions it must win understanding and acceptance of the needs and of the proposed plans for meeting them, from the community at large" (pp. 52–53), one can profit from the hard-won experience of colleagues in the field of primary health care. Some of this was brought into focus by a report (UNICEF–WHO, 1977) based on case studies on community involvement in primary health care in nine countries. No less than twelve factors were there identified and discussed as having proved "favourable to community participation": these included the following:

— Specific government policies to encourage community participation were found to enhance the extent and depth of participation;

— Maximal community participation was achieved when limited local resources were complemented by external resources, especially those provided by the government;

— Specific government programmes for rural and urban development were found to favour community involvement in primary health activities;

— Government administrative decentralization and regional planning appears to have given impetus to community participation;

— The ability of the community to generate activities and participate in them was dependent upon the availability of and the extent to which local resources could be mobilized (these were listed as leaders, personnel, financing and materials);

— Projects and activities where children were the immediate beneficiaries were used as a starting-point for further community efforts.

— Developmental programmes in specific sectors have served as an entry point for the introduction of comprehensive programmes, which have encouraged community participation in wider development activities.

— Non-governmental organization provided channels for community participation.

What must be said unequivocally is that in countries facing daunting problems of economic and technological development, the case for working out at local level—with national and regional advice and support—a viable delivery model for integrated or very closely coordinated services is unanswerable, in terms of scarce resources of both finance and trained personnel. This case is then positively strengthened on tactical grounds by the simple fact that such a "delivery system" is much more likely to be fully used—in all its aspects—than is one which requires mothers and children to deal with a variety, sometimes very bewildering, of agencies and individuals.

Parents and para-professionals

Mittler (*op cit.*, p. 115) stressed that

> the key to better services undoubtedly lies in mobilising the skills and resources of families. The last decade has shown that the development of handicapped children can be actively facilitated by systematic involvement of parents in planning and in delivery programmes of teaching designed to help their children learn specific skills and behaviour. The task for professionals, therefore, is to work in close, active partnerships with families, so that both can not only serve the interests of the child but act as agents of positive change in their own communities.

This brings us naturally to the vast problems of manpower development and appropriate staff training programmes. Mittler cites with approval the current adaptation of the "manpower model" developed by the Canadian Association for Mental Retardation (Roeher, 1978) which in 1981 was being introduced in the Caribbean area.

> This is based on the premise that more than eighty per cent of the people working daily with the handicapped have no formal training (even in the most "advanced" countries) for this work. The task is therefore to find means of bringing them into first-hand contact with recent, relevant methods of training and working with handicapped persons. This can be done only by direct, on-the-spot training in the settings in which they work, rather than by arranging for them to receive lengthy university training in distant centres, whether in their own country or overseas.

The role of external assistance

Given in many countries a near-total absence of indigenous professionals who can provide "on-the-spot" training, what is the appropriate role for various kinds of external assistance? These must meet some down-to-earth criteria in respect of nature, time scale and duration. The "pitfalls to avoid" have been noted by Coombs *et al.* (1973, p. 87), and include:

— adopting imported models without tailoring them to local conditions;

— launching expensive long-term programmes with only a few years of external support in sight;

— depending excessively on expatriate technical assistance experts, and failing to develop competent local personnel to take over from them as quickly as possible;

— constructing, with external assistance, costly and needlessly elaborate facilities that cannot later be replicated using domestic resources alone, and—even worse—that lead to wide dissatisfaction with more modest yet adequate facilities, that the country can afford.

In the study already cited (Heron, 1979, pp. 66–67), it was seen as

. . . essential to recognise the role of the carefully selected adviser in the early stages. I say "carefully-selected" for good reason, since a fairly open request to one of the appropriate UN or other providing sources for "an adviser in the early childhood education field" could all too easily produce the wrong person for that particularly country at that particular stage of its preliminary thinking or planning. Not, I hasten to add, because the various bodies sponsoring technical assistance are careless over such matters: the problem is to find the *right* person who is *available* at the *right* time . . . the first task of an external adviser brought in at an early stage will be of course to learn about the situation and the problems which face the government in the country concerned. That attempted within the limitations of time available, the next step will be to ensure through frank discussion that probably unfamiliar methods and concepts are understood and accepted . . . as being consistent with national objectives and social philosophy. . . . The third stage in the advisory role—if reached—should involve a two-way traffic, planned and supervised jointly by the adviser and one or more senior counterpart professionals, which over a period of years both brings nationals abroad . . . *and* takes experienced but open-minded and innovatory practitioners to the host country, to assist with the early stages of providing the new services, and of *establishing indigenous training facilities*.

This last is the real object of the whole exercise, and what Mittler so rightly identified.

Here it is of interest to quote in full the insight gained in Peru during the development of "non-formal programmes for children", the responsibility for which falls upon the executive bodies at each administrative level of regional and local government, but principally upon the community education centres (Salazar, 1977).

> Experience has shown us that the best non-formal programmes are those in which members of the communities themselves, chosen by their groups, take part as organizers and direct collaborators. They identify with their milieu, its customs, problems, aspirations and language, and are consequently in the best position to carry out efficient work, since they are trusted and respected in their communal groups; this is not so for the teachers, who are often outsiders and have difficulty in integrating in the conditions of these communities.
>
> The auxiliaries have no interest in emigrating to other zones, since, being part of the community, they ensure the continuity and stability of the work undertaken. Having good knowledge of their own community's resources, they are better equipped to exploit this in inexpensive teaching equipment and material. They fulfil their teaching duties with the children efficiently, after receiving suitable training for this purpose, and the more they come to feel motivated the more they wish to take advantage of the opportunities for cultural enrichment which they are given to improve their preparation. They successfully replace teachers in places where it is almost impossible to get specialised staff to come and settle permanently. Finally, they increase the return on the investment made in teaching, since even if they receive some remuneration, it is always less than a teacher's salary—not that this means they are exploited, since they have an opportunity to improve their cultural attainments and financial situation in the course of training for their duties, and taking part in the educational process which affects not only the children but also themselves.

Practical Methods of Intervention

Some programmes originally developed for use in Europe or North America may prove capable of adaptation for use in Third World countries. One example of a home-based, locally monitored training programme to which this may apply is the "Portage Guide to Home Teaching" which has been described in the previous chapter (p. 98). This is currently being adapted and tried in the Caribbean area and in India.

In late 1980, the World Health Organisation (WHO) released, *not* for formal publication but for a two-year trial in several developing countries, the second draft of *An Experimental Manual for Rehabilitation and Disability Prevention for Developing Countries* (Helander, Mendis and Nelson, 1980). This describes for the whole spectrum of major disability

> a set of new approaches. The process of rehabilitation has been de-mystified by breaking it up into component parts, each of which is described in such a way that rehabilitation can safely and effectively be carried out by lay persons, such as a family member or a friend of the disabled, or by the disabled persons themselves. Components with evaluation sheets form training packages, and these have been arranged in six different booklets for the six major disablements dealt with here, i.e. moving, seeing, hearing and speaking, learning, fits and strange behaviour. The manual . . . also includes guides and other information dealing with the entire system for implementing rehabilitation. In addition, it deals with many aspects of disability prevention in the community. *Preventive action is most important, as it may reduce the incidence of disability by at least 50 per cent, or postpone it for many years.* (Our italics).

In Booklet III, "for the training of persons who have difficulty in learning", there are seven "training packages", each accompanied by a short evaluation questionnaire. These packages are for: (i) a mother of a disabled baby: *Breast Feeding*; (ii) a family member of a person who because of learning difficulty needs training in *Looking After Her/Himself* (separate sections for children and for adults); (iii) a family member of a disabled child: *Play Activities* (for children *not* going to school). These are followed by four more packages for family members of a person who has difficulty in learning: (iv) *Schooling* (for school-age children *not* at school, and for unschooled adults); (v) *Social Activities*; (vi) *Daily Tasks*; (vii) *Job Placement* (if above school-age and *not* doing a job or a household task).

The training manuals are at present in $8\frac{1}{2}'' \times 11''$ (approx. 22×28 cm.) format, with itemized instructions almost always illustrated by simple line drawings. This WHO initiative was warmly commended at the Fifth Asian Conference on Mental Retardation, held at Hong Kong in December 1981, and it seems likely that the version to be formally published after the current field trials will find an important place in the resources available to both families and on-the-spot trainers. It is certainly not far-fetched to speculate that its uses will become obvious in the more sophisticated, but still ill-equipped, so-called "developed countries".

This leads directly to the wider implications of this relatively recent turning of attention to the problems faced by Third World countries. The sheer necessity for getting down to the basics, for utilizing the available resources of family and community, for emphasizing the role of what the Canadian "manpower Model" calls the "level one worker"—all this constitutes a fresh challenge to our own "Western" (or "Northern") assumptions about how to meet the needs of the intellectually impaired child or adult. In his "overview" of the 1981 Hong Kong Conference, Mittler spelt out this challenge.

Having just mentioned examples from several countries of "a little training going a long way", he went on:

> Examples such as this confront us with a challenge to some of our most cherished assumptions. Assumptions about expertise and professionalism: that those who have the longest training have the most to offer; that specialisation is a guarantee of expertise and that the professional has more to offer than the person who has 24 hour involvement with the problem. No one is saying that these assumptions are wrong; only that they need reassessment. They need reassessment because it is quite clear from the most highly developed countries that there will never be enough specialists to make anything more than the smallest impact and because we have learned that the highly trained professional must in future share and communicate his skills to others—to parents and families, to volunteers, to paid staff without training or qualifications. We must learn to give away what skills we have—indeed, learning to give away our skills is one of the most difficult skills that we ourselves have to learn, and that we shall have to teach future generations of our students to learn.
>
> Learning to give away skills demands not only a certain skill in working with others but also a considerable personal and professional self-sacrifice. Those who are highly trained are usually highly respected in most societies and enjoy enhanced status. How can we ensure that high status and value can also come from the sharing of one's skills with others?
>
> I have concentrated on the needs of "level one workers" because they have received least attention so far and because they may not be as difficult to meet as is sometimes imagined, provided we develop a systematic and strategic approach to the provision of continuous, short term practical and skill based training using a pyramid principle whereby those who have been trained assume a contractual commitment to become trainers of others in their turn. But if this is to happen, the training and re-training of higher levels of staff assumes an even greater importance.
>
> I will . . . argue provocatively that it may be useful to start from the position that we are all unqualified and ill-equipped to respond to the challenges of the 1980s; we all need a continuous programme of

in-service on the job practical training, and opportunities to advance our knowledge as well as our skills. So much has happened that it is impossible to keep up with the information; we badly need help in learning new techniques relevant to our own culture and society, and in adapting methods and materials that have been developed in other places.

The Future

For too long we have regarded people with intellectual or multiple impairments as forming an almost inevitable part of a category, usually labelled "chronically sick". Because of that, little has been done to reduce the probability of impairment becoming disability. The lack, inadequacy or inappropriateness of intervention has then led inexorably to handicap. We now are beginning to realize that this is not wholly or even mainly because of ignorance, or of a general shortage of trained professionals—though we shall always need more, of the right kind. The basic obstacle has been—and continues to be—one of *attitude*. That will have to be overcome in differing cultures in differing ways; but the universal challenge is to be positive instead of negative or apathetic. The battle against handicap can only be fought successfully by persuading everyone—parents, relatives, neighbours, professionals, administrators, planners, politicians—that the consequences of intellectual impairment *can* be significantly limited by timely and appropriate positive action.

References

Bank-Mikkelsen, N. E. (1977). "Changing Patterns in Residential Services for the Mentally Retarded". Copenhagen: National Board of Social Service.

Bellamy, G. T., Horner, R. H. and Inman, D. P. (1979). "Vocational Habilitation of Severely Retarded Adults". Baltimore: University Park Press.

Belmont, L. (Ed.) (1981). Severe mental retardation across the world: epidemiological studies. *International Journal of Mental Health*, **10** (1), 3–119.

Billis, J. (1981). "Project in Adult Education for Mentally Handicapped Students". Reference document, Metropolitan Region, Royal MENCAP, London (mimeo).

*Cherniss, C. (1980). "Staff Burnout: Job Stress in the Human Services". London: Sage.

Chigier, E. (1975). "Use of Group Techniques in the Rehabilitation of the Retarded in Israel". Paper presented at Fifth Pan-Pacific Rehabilitation Conference, Singapore (mimeo).

Coombs, P. H., *et al.* (1973). "New Paths to Learning for Rural Children and Youth". New York: International Council for Educational Development.

Croton, G. (1980). " 'Let's Go . . . . ': an account of the BBC's Mental Handicap Project, 1976–9". London: British Broadcasting Corporation.

Cunningham, C. C. and Sloper, P. (1977). Parents of Down's Syndrome babies: their early needs. *Child: care, health and development*, **3**, 325–347.

Department of Education and Science (1978a). "Special educational needs". Report of the committee of enquiry into the education of handicapped children and young people (The Warnock Committee). London: HMSO.

Department of Education and Science (1978b). "The Libraries' Choice". London: HMSO.

DHSS (1976). "Fit for the Future". Report of the Committee on Child Health Services (Chairman, Prof. S. D. M. Court) (*Cmnd 6684*). London: HMSO.

DHSS (1981). "Adult Residential Accommodation". Mental Health Buildings Evaluation Programme, Report S8. London: DHSS Works Group, Branch Dev. 3.2.

Dickson, M. E. A. (1976). Voluntary service by the mentally handicapped. *REAP*, **2** (2), 130–137.

Dybwad, G. (1970). Treatment of the mentally retarded: a cross-national view. *In* "Socio-cultural Aspects of Mental Retardation" (Ed. H. C. Haywood). New York: Appleton-Century-Crofts.

Edgerton, R. B. (1970). Mental retardation in non-Western societies: toward a cross-cultural perspective on incompetence. *In* "Social-cultural Aspects of Mental Retardation" (Ed. H. C. Haywood). New York: Appleton-Century-Crofts.

Edgerton, R. B. (1981). Another look at culture and mental retardation. *In* "Psychological Influences in Retarded Performance" (Eds M. J. Begab, H. C. Haywood and H. L. Garber), Vol. 1. Baltimore: University Park Press.

Evans, R. K. and Green, J. M. (1979). "Honeylands: The Exeter Resource Centre for Handicapped Children and Their Families: An Independent Evaluation Through Interviews with User and Non-user Parents". Exeter: Paediatric Research Unit, Royal Devon and Exeter Hospital (mimeo).

Firth, H. (1982). The effectiveness of parent workshops in a mental handicap service. *Child: care, health and development, 8*, 77–91.

Flynn, R. J. and Nitsch, K. E. (Eds) (1981). "Normalisation, Social Integration and Community Services". Baltimore: University Park Press.

Gath, A. (1978). "Down's Syndrome and the Family: the Early Years". London and New York: Academic Press.

Gold, M. (1973). Research on the vocational habilitation of the retarded: the present, the future. *In* "International Review of Research in Mental Retardation" (Ed. N. Ellis), Vol. 6. New York and London: Academic Press.

Gold, M. (1975). Vocational training. *In* "Mental Retardation and Developmental Disabilities" (Ed. J. Wortis), Vol. VII. New York: Brunner Mazel.

Gottlieb, J. (1981). Mainstreaming: fulfilling the promise? *American Journal of Mental Deficiency, 86* (2), 115–126.

Green, J. M. and Evans, R. K. (1981). Honeylands' role in the pre-school years, I: developing a relationship. *Child: care, health and development, 8*, 21–38.

Grunewald, K. (1974). "The Mentally Retarded in Sweden". Stockholm: The Swedish Institute.

Gunzburg, H. C. (1973). Thirty-nine steps leading towards normalised living practices in living units for the mentally handicapped. *British Journal of Mental Subnormality, 19*, 91–99.

Hall, V. and Russell, O. (1980). A national survey of community nursing services for the mentally handicapped. *Mental Handicap Studies Research Reports*, No. 10. Bristol: The University.

Helander, E., Mendis, P. and Nelson,G. (1980). "Training the Disabled in the Community: An Experimental Manual on Rehabilitation and Disability Prevention for Developing Countries". Geneva: World Health Organisation.

Heron, A. (1979). Planning Early Childhood Care and Education in Developing Countries. Paris: UNESCO International Institute for Educational Planning.

Heron, A., Kebbon, L., Ericsson, K. and Blunden, R. (1981). Evaluation of services for mentally handicapped persons: symposium on recent studies in Sweden and Britain. *In* "Frontiers of Knowledge in Mental Retardation. (Ed. P. Mittler), Vol. 1. Baltimore: University Park Press.

Jeffree, D. (1979). The "PATH" Project. APEX, *J. of Brit. Inst. of Mental Handicap*, **7** (3), 91–93.

Jeffree, D. and McConkey, R. (1976). "Let Me Speak". London: Souvenir Press.

Jeffree, D., McConkey, R. and Hewson, S. (1977a). "Teaching the Handicapped Child". London: Souvenir Press.

Jeffree, D., McConkey, R. and Hewson, S. (1977b). "Let Me Play". London: Souvenir Press.

King's Fund Centre (1980). "An Ordinary Life: Comprehensive Locally-based Residential Services for Mentally Handicapped People". London: King's Fund Centre.

Klein, L. (1979). Heath Croft—a force for good. *Community Care*, 10 May, pp. 17–18.

Kuh, D. (1978). *Review of the technique "Program Analysis of Service Systems", (PASS)*. Exeter: The University, Institute of Biometry and Community Medicine (mimeo).

Libby, M. (1981). "Meaning Well . . . and Thinking Right". Report of a visit to North America on behalf of the Leonard Cheshire Foundation (mimeo).

Lippmann, L. and Goldberg, I. I. (1973). "Right to Education". New York: Teachers College Press.

Loos, F. and Tizard, J. (1955). The employment of adult imbeciles in a hospital workshop. *American Journal of Mental Deficiency*, **59**, 395–403.

Maslow, A. H. (1968). "Towards a Psychology of Being". (2nd Edn) New York: Van Nostrand.

Mathieson, S. and Blunden, R. (1980). NIMROD is piloting a course towards community life. *Health and Social Service Journal*, 25 January, 122–124.

MENCAP (1981). *The Pathway Scheme*. London: Royal Society for Mentally Handicapped Children and Adults.

Mittler, P. (1979). People Not Patients: Problems and Policies in Mental Handicap". London: Methuen.

Moss, J. W. (1979). Postsecondary Vocational Education for Mentally Retarded Adults. Reston, Virginia: ERIC Clearinghouse on Handicapped and Gifted Children.

National Development Group for the Mentally Handcapped (1976). Pamphlet No. 1: *Mental handicap—planning together*. London: DHSS.

National Development Group for the Mentally Handicapped (1977a). Pamphlet No. 2: *Mentally handicapped children—a plan for action*. London: DHSS.

National Development Group for the Mentally Handicapped (1977b). Pamphlet No. 3: *Helping mentally handicapped school-leavers*. London: DHSS.

National Development Group for the Mentally Handicapped (1977c). Pamphlet No. 4: *Residential short-term care for mentally handicapped people—suggestions for action*. London: DHSS.

National Development Group for the Mentally Handicapped (1977d). Pamphlet No. 5: *Day services for mentally handicapped adults*. London: DHSS.

National Development Group for the Mentally Handicapped (1978). *Helping mentally handicapped people in hospital—a report to the Secretary of State for Social Services*. London: DHSS.

Newson, J. and Newson, E. (1976). Parental roles and social contexts. *In* "The Organisation and Impact of Social Research" (Ed. M. Shipman). London: Routledge and Kegan Paul.

Nirje, B. (1970). The normalisation principle: implications and comments. *British Journal of Mental Subnormality*, **16** (2).

Oswin, M. (1978). "Children Living in Long-stay Hospitals". London: Spastics International Medical Publications/Heinemann Medical Books.

Oswin, M. (1981). "Bereavement and Mentally Handicapped People". London: King's Fund Centre.

Plank, M. (1982). "Teams for Mentally Handicapped People". London: The Campaign for Mentally Handicapped People.

Porter, F. (1978). "The Pilot Parent Program". Omaha, Nebraska: Greater Omaha Association for Retarded Citizens.

Pugh, G. and Russell, P. (1977. "Shared Care: Support Services for Families with Handicapped Children". London: National Children's Bureau.

Radel, M. S. (1980). *The Family Education Unit—where are we now?* Paper presented to 16th National Conference, Australian Group for the Scientific Study of Mental Deficiency.

Raynes, N. V., Pratt, M. W. and Roses, S. (1979). "Organisational Structure and the Care of the Mentally Retarded". London: Croom Helm.

Richardson, A. and Wisbeach, A. (1976). "I Can Use My Hands". London: The Toy Libraries Association.

Roeher, A. (1978). Models of staff training. *In* "Choices: proceedings of 7th World Congress on Mental Handicap (International League of Societies for the Mentally Handicapped)" (Ed. H. Spudich). Vienna: Lebenshilfe.

Rosenau, N. and Provencal, G. (1981). Community placement and parental misgivings. *Mental Retardation*, **31** (2), 3–11.

Rowan, P. (1980). "What Sort of Life?" Windsor, England: NFER Publishing Company.

Salazar, J. C. I. (1977). Non-formal education programmes for children and parents in Peru. *Prospects*, **7** (4), 549–556.

Shearer, A. (1972). *Our life: a conference report*. London: Campaign for the Mentally Handicapped.

Shearer, M. and Shearer, D. E. (1972). The Portage Project: a model for early childhood education. *Exceptional Child*, **36**, 210–217.

UNICEF–WHO (1977). *Community involvement in primary health care: a study of the process of community motivation and continued participation*. Report JC 21/UNICEF–WHO/77.2, Rev. 2. Geneva: WHO.

Weinberg, M. (1981). Pengwern. *Parents Voice* (Royal MENCAP Journal), **31** (1), 13–14.

Welsh Office (1978). NIMROD: *Report of a joint working party on the provision of a community-based mental handicap service in South Glamorgan*. Cardiff: The Welsh Office.

Wertheimer, A. (1981). "Living for the Present: Older Parents with a Mentally Handicapped Person Living at Home". London: Campaign for Mentally Handicapped People.

Williams, P. and Shoultz, B. (1982). "We Can Speak for Ourselves". London: Souvenir Press.

Wolfensberger, W. (1972). "The Principle of Normalisation in Human Services". Toronto: National Institute for Mental Retardation.

Wolfensberger, W. (1977). "A Balanced Multi-component Advocacy/ Protection Scheme". Toronto: Canadian Association for the Mentally Retarded.

Wolfensberger, W. and Glenn, L. (1975). "Program Analysis of Service Systems (PASS 3)". Toronto: National Institute for Mental Retardation.

Wolfensberger, W. and Zanha, H. (Eds) (1973). "Citizen Advocacy and Protective Services for the Impaired and Handicapped". Toronto: National Institute for Mental Retardation.

World Health Organisation (1980). "International Classification of Impairments, Disabilities and Handicaps". Geneva: World Health Organisation.

Appendix I

E.R.G. Reports, Nos 1–13, 1977–1981

1. *The Sheffield Development Project on Services for the Mentally Handicapped: implementation of the Feasibility Study recommendations.* Alastair Heron and Janet Phillips (1977).
2. *Staff attitudes and activities in adult training centres.* Gina Armstrong, Alastair Heron and David Race (1977).
3. *Voluntary services for the mentally handicapped.* Nigel A. Malin and Deborah Race (1977).
4. *Residential services for mentally handicapped adults: interim report on Stage One.* Nigel Malin and David Race (1979).
5. *The role and function of the social services department in the total system of provision for the mentally handicapped.* Gina Armstrong, David Race and Deborah Race (1979).
6. *The Woodside Assessment Unit.* Adela de Gonzales and Alastair Heron (1980).
7. *A study of change in adult training centres 1977–1979.* Gina Armstrong, Alastair Heron and Isobel Todd (1980).
8. *Mentally handicapped under-fives: Leeds and Sheffield services as seen by parents.* Gina Armstrong, Glenys Jones, Deborah Race and Jacky Ruddock (1980).
9. *Group homes for mentally handicapped adults.* Nigel Malin (1980).
10. *Short-term care for the mentally handicapped: a study of availability and use.* Isobel Todd and Alastair Heron (1980).
11. *The Ryegate Centre.* Glenys Jones, Jacky Ruddock and Alastair Heron (1981).
12. *Residential services for mentally handicapped adults: Stage Two.* Nigel Malin (1981).
13. *Mentally handicapped school-leavers: a follow-up study.* Alastair Heron (1981).

Notes

(a) Several complete sets of these reports are held by the Library, The University, Sheffield S10 2TN, England, and a further complete set by the British Library, Lending Division, Boston Spa, Wetherby, West Yorkshire, LS23 7BQ, England.

(b) Variable numbers of copies of individual reports are in stock c/o The Secretary, Department of Psychology, The University, Sheffield S10 2TN, England. These are available free on request until stocks are exhausted: they will *not* be reprinted. Reimbursement of postal charges will be requested.

169

Appendix II: Further Reading

Bayley, M. (1973). "Mental handicap and community care: a study of mentally handicapped people in Sheffield". London: Routledge and Kegan Paul.

Bricker, D., Seibert, J. M. and Casuso, V. (1980). Early intervention. *In* "Advances in Mental Handicap Research" (Eds J. Hogg and P Mittler), Vol. 1. Chichester: Wiley.

Clarke, A. D. B. and Mittler, P. (Eds) (1980). *Mental retardation: prevention, amelioration and service delivery*. (Report of the joint commission, International Association for the Scientific Study of Mental Deficiency/International League of Societies for Mentally Handicapped Persons). Brussels: ILSMHP, rue Forestière 13.

Connolly, K. J. and Prechtl, H. F. R. (Eds) (1982). *Maturation and development—biological and psychological perspectives*. London: Heinemann.

Craft, M. and Craft, A. (1978). "Sex and the Mentally Handicapped". London: Routledge and Kegan Paul.

Department of Health and Social Security (1979). "Report of the Committee of Enquiry into Mental Handicap Nursing and Care" (Chairman: Peggy Jay) (Commd. 7468-I). London: HMSO.

Dybwad, Rosemary F. (Ed.) (1979). "International Directory of Mental Retardation Resources", 2nd Edn (revised). Brussels: ILSMH, rue Forestière 13.

International Union for Child Welfare (1981). *Mental Retardation, the Child and his Surroundings*. (Occasional Papers, No. 1). Geneva: IUCW.

Locker, D., Rao, B. and Weddell, J. M. (1979a). Knowledge of and attitudes towards mental handicap: their implications for community care. *Community Medicine*, **1** (2), 127–136.

Locker, D. (1979b). Public acceptance of community care for the mentally handicapped. *APEX*, **7** (2), 44–46.

Malin, N., Race, D. and Jones, G. (1980). *Services for the mentally handicapped in Britain*. London: Croom Helm.

National Institute on Mental Retardation (Canada) (1978). "Residential Services: Community Housing Options for Handicapped People", 2nd Edn. Toronto: NIMR.

National Institute on Mental Retardation (Canada) (1979). "A Formative Evaluation of the Southern Alberta ComServ E. and D. Project". Toronto: Canadian Association for Mental Retardation.

O'Connor, G. (1976). "Home is a Good Place". AAMD Monograph No. 2. Washington: American Association for Mental Deficiency.

Perske, R. and Perske, M. (1980). "New Life in the Neighbourhood". Nashville, Tennessee: Abingdon.

Plog, S. C. and Santamour, M. B. (Eds) (1980). "The Year 2000 and Mental Retardation". London: Plenum.

President's Committee on Mental Retardation (PCMR) (1975). "Mental Retardation: The Known and Unknown".

President's Committee on Mental Retardation (PCMR) (1976a). "Mental Retardation: Century of Decision—(Report to the President)".

President's Committee on Mental Retardation (PCMR) (1976b). "Mental Retardation: Trends in State Services".

President's Committee on Mental Retardation (PCMR) (1976c). "Changing Patterns in Residential Services for the Mentally Retarded". Revised edition.

President's Committee on Mental Retardation (PCMR) (1977). "Mental Retardation: Past and Present". (MR76).

President's Committee on Mental Retardation (PCMR) (1978a). "Mental Retardation and the Future".

President's Committee on Mental Retardation (PCMR) (1978b). "Mental Retardation: the Leading Edge Service Programs That Work". (Report to the President).

President's Committee on Mental Retardation (PCMR) (1980). "Mental Retardation: Prevention Strategies That Work". Washington, D.C.: US Government Printing Office.

Race, D. G. and Race, D. M. (1979). "The Cherries Group Home—A Beginning". London: HMSO.

Roos, P., McCann, B. M. and Addison, M. R. (Eds) (1980). "Shaping the Future: Community-based Residential Services and Facilities for Mentally Retarded People". Baltimore: University Park Press.

Ryan, J. (with Thomas, F.) (1980). "The Politics of Mental Handicap". Harmondsworth, Penguin Books.

Shearer, A. (1981a). "Disability: Whose Handicap?". Oxford: Blackwell.

Shearer, A. (1981b). "Bringing Mentally Handicapped Children Out of Hospital". London: King's Fund Centre.

Strain, P. S. and Kerr, M. M. (1981). "Mainstreaming of Children in Schools". New York and London: Academic Press.

Tizard, J. (1970). The role of social institutions in the causation, prevention and alleviation of mental retardation. In "Social-cultural Aspects of Mental Retardation" (Ed. H. C. Haywood). New York: Appleton-Century-Crofts, pp. 281–340.

UNESCO (1980). "Handicapped Children: Early Detection, Intervention and Education". Paris: Unesco ED/MD/63.

Whelan, E. and Speake, B. (1979). "Learning to Cope". London: Souvenir Press.

Wilkin, D. (1979). "Caring for the Mentally Handicapped Child". London: Croom Helm.

Author Index

Subject Index